Systems Convening

A crucial form of leadership for the 21st century

Etienne and Beverly Wenger-Trayner

First published in 2021 by

Social Learning Lab

The Social Learning Lab is a project of Wenger-Trayner Unip. LDA.
Rua da Bela Vista 2
Sesimbra 2970-621
Portugal
https://wenger-trayner.com

ISBN: 978-989-53290-1-4 (downloadable PDF)
ISBN: 978-989-53290-0-7 (printed version)

Book designed by Ade Popoola
Book cover by Andrea Morgado

Contents

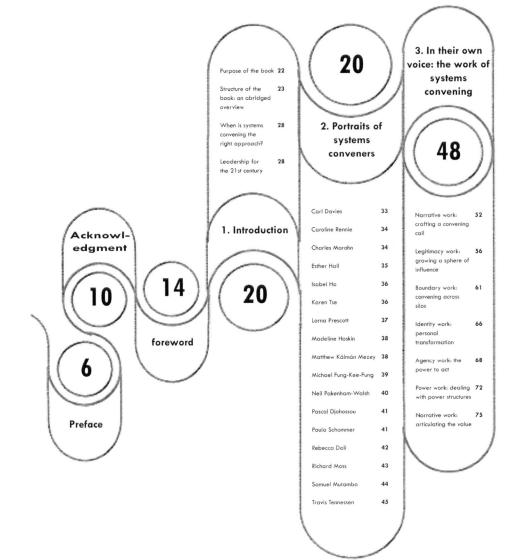

5. Conclusion

106

Annex

110

112

80

References

116

4. The essence of systems
convening: a more
theoretical look

Index

Preface

The journey of this book started in 2018 with an email from Jenny Oppenheimer of the Lankelly Chase Foundation in the UK:

> *Dear Bev and Etienne,*
>
> *I've been introduced to your work by Matthew Mezey of the Health Foundation.*
>
> *…*
>
> *We do not consider ourselves a traditional funder, rather we work as a facilitator and a convener and aim to be smart and imaginative about the actions we take.*
>
> *…*
>
> *Developing a systemic response to people with severe and multiple disadvantages involves working and convening in complex environments and your thinking and work on this is inspiring. I wonder if there might be an opportunity for us to explore this in greater depth?*
>
> *…*
>
> *Jenny*

The ensuing conversations led to an invitation to run a workshop in London sponsored by Lankelly Chase and bringing together funders and practitioners from different U.K. organizations. Matthew Mezey attended the workshop, approaching us at the end to urge us to write a small book about our take on systems convening. While it had been our intention to write more about it in a future book, it was not at the top of our list of writing projects. In the spirit of convening, Matthew and Jenny suggested they could gather a group of organizations to chip in enough funding make it a top priority.

A few months later they had done it. Lankelly Chase, the Centre for Public Impact, and the Royal Society of Arts agreed to join in supporting the writing. And every few months for the last year, we have met with Jenny Oppenheimer, Shaheen Warren, and Ian Burbidge from these organizations as well as Matthew Mezey and Benjamin Taylor of RedQuadrant to discuss the book and its progress. Hence a book about systems convening was brought into being through a process of convening.

Our interest in systems convening does not spring from systems theory, even if there are many parallels. Rather our trajectory is an evolution of our work on social learning theory and practice, which started in the late '80s with the focus on communities of practice. While our consulting work had traditionally been with clients cultivating communities of practice,[1] we were increasingly invited to advise about enabling learning in multi-stakeholder, multi-scaled, and multi-practice situations. In 2014, we wrote about this as learning across practices in what we called *landscapes of practice*.[2] In the same book, we wrote about our experience with clients who were transforming their landscape by leading complex social-learning projects. We identified their work as a particular kind of cross-boundary leadership we called *systems convening*. In response to this writing, we received a significant number of emails from people writing to share their joy at being "discovered" and given a name for what they were doing. Many said it made them cry. We knew we were onto something.

Our first intention in this current book was to sharpen our articulation of the role and practice of *systems conveners*. After carrying out around 40 interviews with people doing this kind of work in very different contexts, often as a team, and under many different roles, we started to focus more on systems convening as an approach. Delving deeper into its nature, we saw that it could even more broadly be adopted as a perspective that allows a person in any role, or taking any approach, to bring certain kinds of questions to their endeavor.

As an approach and a perspective, systems convening is made increasingly relevant by the twin trends of globalization and fragmentation and their manifestations at all levels of scale. Our focus on it was inspired by people who care to make a difference to challenges with multiple moving parts in socially complex contexts. These kinds of contexts have risen in salience with unfolding events such as the global health crisis brought about by COVID-19, the results of environmental emergencies, or the increase in refugees and people fleeing forced displacements. Our hope is that we are making a contribution to these twenty-first century problems by articulating the kind of work some people have taken on, often in the shadows, to bring about the type of big and small changes that will add up to making a sustainable and transformative difference.

---

1 See Wenger, 1998.
2 See Wenger-Trayner and Wenger-Trayner, 2014.

Centre for Public Impact

At the Centre for Public Impact, we know that government can't solve 21st century challenges with 20th century tools and systems. That's why we have an emerging vision to reimagine government so that it works for everyone. A global not-for-profit organisation founded by the Boston Consulting Group, we serve as a learning partner for governments, public servants and the diverse network of changemakers leading the charge to reimagine government — holding space to collectively make sense of the complex challenges we face, and drive meaningful change through experimentation.

RSA

We are the RSA. The royal society for arts, manufactures and commerce. We're committed to a future that works for everyone. A future where we can all participate in its creation. The RSA has been at the forefront of significant social impact for over 250 years. Our proven change process, rigorous research, innovative ideas platforms, and diverse global community of over 30,000 problem solvers, deliver solutions for lasting change. We invite you to be part of this change. Join our community. Together, we'll unite people and ideas to resolve the challenges of our time. Find out more at thersa.org.

Lankelly Chase

Lankelly Chase is an independent foundation striving for a world healed by justice, equity and inclusion. A world where all people can live with dignity and opportunity in supportive communities. Our mission is to challenge injustice and create the conditions for much healthier systems to emerge. We support action in the UK that reveals, questions, dismantles systems that do harm, or seeks to heal, reimagines and transforms systems that fundamentally shift patterns of perspectives, power, and participation. This work seeks to honour and build upon the work and wisdom of others past and present.

Acknowledgments

Thank you to all the people who have inspired us to think and write about systems conveners, systems convening, and a systems convening perspective. Your work has enriched our lives and, more directly, the lives of the people involved in your convening endeavors.

Thank you to all those we interviewed. If your words found their way into the book, you are introduced in Section 2. Even if we do not have a direct quote from you in the text, every conversation we had helped shaped the ideas and words that found their way into the book. This includes: Alfredo del Valle, Ann Hendrix-Jenkins, Florencia Guerzovich, Jane Pightling, J.D. Brown, John Hoven, Kaliya Identity Woman, Laurel Whistler, Massimo Curatella, Nathalie Creary, Orit Gal, Patrick Hoverstadt, Phoebe Tickell, Richard D. Bartlett, Ross Hall, Scott David, Stefan Groenendal, Stephen Johnston, and Thea Snow.

Some of you introduced us to other systems conveners whom we otherwise wouldn't have known. We are grateful in particular to Ann Hendrix-Jenkins and Scott David who made sure we included the voices of systems conveners who would otherwise not be in our networks.

Thanks to our sponsors, who joined us for regular calls to keep updated with the book. We are sorry not to keep Shaheen Warren of the Centre for Public Impact as our project manager forever. Jenny Oppenheimer of Lankelly Chase was the one who made the connections and kept conversation grounded. Ian Burbidge of the Royal Society of Art, Manufactures and Commerce was a good listening ear and kept us going with his comment: "I wish I had known this before I ever started out." Also on the team meetings were Matthew Mezey and Benjamin Taylor, who put us in touch with lots of people, pointed us to relevant readings, and whose careful comments and edits have made this a better book. Thank you to Rob Worth, Editor in Chief at Exapt Press, who helped with some last-minute corrections.

We are also indebted to the people who joined our first systems convening workshop, even before the conceptualization was complete: Frauke Godat, Laurel Hammond, Laurel Whistler, Laurie Robinson, Olga Vtorushina, Piret Jeedas, Tiago Duarte as well as Caroline Rennie and Travis Tennessen whose voices appear in the book. They all shared their projects for discussion, and the group used these reflections to think through some of our emerging ideas for the book.

Acknowledgment

We also thank the people in the Systems Convening discussion group,[1] an open group with around 120 members who joined to discuss systems convening.

We have greatly benefited from our work with all of you and we hope that this is only a start.

Etienne and Bev

---

3 https://groups.io/g/20SysConv/topics

Foreword

As a Provost, I can point to the work of program advisory boards, of our centers and institutes, field research, internships, and service learning projects as evidence of our university's connection to improving conditions within our community. However, in recent years, even the most community-centered colleges and universities have been bedeviled by the shifting socio-economic landscape. It has influenced our operations, with rapid technological advancements that simultaneously impact the professions and how we prepare students for them. It has also raised disruptive health and safety concerns that do not respect borders. To respond to the complex problems that plague our communities, while adapting to the cumulative effects of these conditions on the university, there is a need for university leaders to both learn from and work with corporate, governmental, and non-profit leaders in new ways.

Beverly and Etienne highlight an advanced approach to enabling cooperation among institutions in order to strengthen communities. Their description of the role, mindset, and methods of systems conveners enabled me as an academic leader to identify new areas of focus. I believe these will help foster shared purpose across organizational boundaries, elicit curriculum suggestions from employers and other stakeholder groups, and enable us to work more collaboratively across institutions to design more robust learning ecosystems.

Christopher L. Washington Ph.D.

Executive Vice President and Provost
Franklin University

There's a variation on a Kurt Lewin quote that goes "if you want to truly understand the world, try to change it."

I've been an internal change agent in a big system for more than three decades and through everyday experiences of leading change, I can see and feel how much our world is changing. We are moving to a world where people are connecting all the time, where digital media and social channels are no longer distractions; they are central to the functioning of society. A world where power and authority are less about position in the formal system and more about the trusting relationships we build by collaborating and sharing. A world where enabling change is less about planning a change process, programme management and governance systems and more about connecting, convening and building bridges with and between many people.

So yes, systems convening is a crucial form of leadership for the 21st century and I welcome the contribution that Bev and Etienne are making through this book.

Let's answer their convening call. The more we mobilise people around the potential for a radically different future, the better we prepare for the future.

Helen Bevan

Chief Transformation Officer
NHS Horizons

Health and social care across Surrey is undergoing a major transformation as we work towards a more integrated, preventative and whole-population model of service delivery. Vital to that transformation will be a number of "Systems Conveners," whose roles are intended to both stimulate radical change and increase its pace. This is a new concept to many. However, *Systems convening: A crucial form of leadership for the 21st century* has been an invaluable tool, which has helped us understand how to create a space to enable systems convening to thrive.

Health and social care in Surrey operates across Surrey County Council, Surrey-based NHS organisations, as well as an extensive provider network. In order to achieve our goals of reducing health inequality and greater system integration, we need to be able to make sense of what is often a very complex web of connections. This is a hugely challenging task, but it is precisely the kind of situation which calls for a systems convener.

The recognition of that, along with the creation and fulfilment of these roles across Surrey is truly pioneering. As outlined in this new book, post-holders will work across constituent parts of the system, "reconfiguring boundaries and identities, [giving] the attention to delicate issues of agency and power, and the process of making visible the value, sometimes obvious and often subtle, created for participants and other stakeholders." There will also be a need for "combining processes of engagement, imagination, and alignment and leveraging their complementarity." As Simon White, Executive Director of Adult Social Care for Surrey County Council says, "We are not looking for… heroic individuals who can do what we cannot do ourselves. The vision for the future and the ability to deliver it rests with us, working as a system."

Jude Middleton

Project Manager, Transforming Outcomes for People
Surrey County Council

This is the hour, the day, the year, the century for systems conveners. As we face down climate change and social justice challenges, the leadership described in this book is both worthy and elusive. A bow to the authors, sponsors and the conveners who spotlight the role.

Systems conveners and Liberating Structures practitioners focus attention on the relationships among the parties in contrast to the parts themselves. They span and broker and bridge-build and weave across boundaries, inclusively shaping solutions in the space between. They attune to the deep embeddedness of system nested in system, nested in system, ad infinitum. They delight in unearthing the unexamined interdependencies and hidden opportunities that arise as convening unfolds over time. It is leadership requiring a long view of the future, while unleashing action in the present.

Productive convening work is guided by a shared social need to make a difference and a series of self discoveries made possible in the context of a group—an ensemble of people with very different backgrounds. I applaud all leaders who choose to walk through the door labeled "systems convener." There is no end in sight in regard to what we need to learn. See you on the other side!

Keith McCandless

Co-author, The Surprising Power of Liberating Structures – Simple Rules to Unleash a Culture of Innovation

With this book, Etienne and Beverly Wenger-Trayner offer a valuable contribution to the world and the leadership community by outlining characteristics necessary for modern leadership: the ability to nurture and support what we in complexity leadership call, adaptive space. Adaptive space can be thought of as the conditions that promote adaptability. It does this by creating safe spaces for agents (people, ideas, resources, information, technology) to "conflict" and "connect." Conflicting, as the authors so elegantly identify, is the creative force that allows new ideas and innovations to develop and morph into adaptive solutions to complex problems. Connecting is the emergent force that allows innovative solutions to amplify and scale into an adaptive new order for people, organizations, and society.

While systems convening is referred to in the book as social learning leadership and developed from that discipline, what the authors have discovered is so much more. Systems convening reveals and elaborates the fundamental dynamics through which social systems naturally adapt and survive in response to changing environments. Systems convening brings together many of the core dynamics of complexity as shown in the physical and biological sciences and combines it with deep knowledge and awareness of social systems and human nature. While academic literature has provided the outlines of how these processes and dynamics occur, systems convening fills in the blanks. It provides the most complete resource to my knowledge of what systems convening, or enabling leaders in complexity leadership, must do to create and foster adaptive space. As we now so painstakingly know, this skill is no longer just a "nice to have" but a "must have" for leaders and followers challenged to survive and thrive in an ever-increasingly complex world.

Mary Uhl-Bien, Ph.D.

BNSF Railway Endowed Professor of Leadership
Neeley School of Business, TCU

Our communities are living systems, not machines. Through a constant process of discovery and creating, everything is constantly changing. Always unpredictable, always seeking the best expression of an identity that works. For too long, this unpredictability has driven us to mechanistic control of life's inherently messy dynamics. As if we could capture and erase unintended consequences of the wrong kind; as if we could make life submit to our will through command and control. Today, it has become impossible to deny this unpredictability. The interconnection and interdependence of the dynamics of life are on display everywhere. From the COVID-19 pandemic, to financial markets, from climate change to social networks. As we try to heal the damage our Cartesian-Newtonian worldview has wrought, we are increasingly turning to the idea of integration. Seeing the system as a system, and calling it to come together to discover, learn, reflect, create, and become more. And do it again and again in an endless cycle of co-creativity.

But while the language of integration of communities, organisations, institutions and systems is the conversation everywhere, the actions we take to re-create and re-discover the life of our communities are stuck in the past. The methods and processes we have remain hammers and nails. We need a change in how we work together, because the process we use to get to the future is the future we get. We need to move from a process of assembling parts to an invitation that generates a whole. Our identity needs to shift from that of "my role," to that of "our whole." Etienne and Beverly Wenger-Trayner and their companions on this research journey point a way to reimagine the essential capacities and capabilities this time demands. As Peter Block has written, leadership is convening. We have much to learn together. Let's begin.

Myron Rogers

Author, A Simpler Way
Speaker, consultant
Chair, Lankelly Chase Foundation

1

Introduction

You may not have heard about them; what they do is rarely in their job description. You may not even be aware of what they do; they tend to act as enablers rather than taking credit or seeking the spotlight. But they are here—working on sustainable change, across challenging silos, in complex social landscapes, amid changing circumstances. We call them *systems conveners*.

Their stance is both visionary and pragmatic. They look at the social landscape in which they operate—an organization, a city, a community, a country, the world—and they see unrealized potential that exists across traditional boundaries and silos. Many challenges today require learning that brings people together across different practices, different institutions, different goals, different cultures, different loyalties. Systems conveners seek to enable the conversations and learning across these boundaries that are needed to make a difference.

They can do this because they take on a particular kind of leadership that creates synergies, often between unlikely learning partners. They are interested in doing what it takes to make a real difference, more than in complying with convenient metrics, following strict job descriptions, or making showy moves. They know that most challenges cannot be addressed by one person or even one group. When seeking to make a difference, they are ready to embrace the full complexity of the human world; they are willing to engage the perspectives of all involved to create outcomes that even they wouldn't have expected. They welcome bottom-up initiative as an engine of transformation because they believe that change is more likely to be sustainable when people, and unlikely alliances among them, have an active part in it. Systems conveners play the long game with dogged tenacity. Knowing that real transformation of contexts, cultures, boundaries, and identities takes time, they are prepared to go the distance, moving incrementally through a series of successes and failures.

And we need them more than ever. In world with multiple crises and competing agendas, joining the dots, shifting world views, and becoming more agile is a survival imperative. This is true at all levels of scale; cross-boundary engagement and innovative thinking are required for global challenges as well as local community strengthening.

Purpose of this book

For many people, being a systems convener is only something that exists in retrospect. They may never have set out to convene people across a social landscape but have found themselves taking this on as a way to make a difference they care to make. Even if they set out with the intention to use a convening approach to make a difference, they may not have an adequate language to describe what they do.

The purpose of this book is to shine some light on systems convening—to emphasize the importance of this work and provide a language to articulate what it entails. We also want to describe the experience of people who do it. Systems convening is not an abstract type of work that can be done with detachment. It takes personal commitment and passion. It involves the heart as well as the head. To bring this to life, we have included portraits and quotes from people we interviewed. While the systems conveners we quote speak as individuals, the work is often done as a team.

We hope that shining a light on this work will be useful for those who already do it, for those looking for a way in, and for those who are in a position to sponsor the work—enabling more opportunities for this work to have a transformative impact. If you are a systems convener, we hope that you recognize yourself in these pages and see that you are not alone. We hope you gain some language to describe what you do and find some inspiration from the approaches, practices, and strategies of your peers. If you are a manager or a funder, it is important to be aware of this type of work, what it can contribute, and how it interplays with organizational structures and strategies. Having a language for it will help you figure out how to recognize and support it. Because systems conveners are often mavericks who think out of the box, you need to distinguish them from people who just thrive on wild ideas. Understanding more clearly what systems conveners actually do and the work it really takes will make it easier to see the difference. We hope that this book will help you know whether you need systems conveners, and if you do, how to spot them and make the most of their skills.

At the same time, we recognize that the project of writing about systems conveners requires some caveats and we need to voice some of our reservations. While we have tried to show the hard work and tribulations of systems conveners, we have written a relatively positive description of what we have observed in the people we interviewed and the people we have worked with. There is a danger of romanticizing the idea. We cannot assume that anyone claiming to be a systems convener will live up to the name. We have also experienced people with a tendency to megalomania, narcissism, or delusions of grandeur who, without some scrutiny, could get a free pass to the claim of doing systems convening. But becoming more precise about what counts as systems convening also has its risks. Abstracting it into a job description to motivate and prescribe action is likely to be self-defeating. There is a balance between opening a space in which systems conveners can do their work and specifying what it is that they are expected to do, between enabling an art that is contextual and making it official enough to be recognized. Making systems convening into a thing can also overblow it; this might prevent people who could benefit from the perspective from seeing its relevance because they do not consider themselves full-fledge systems conveners. Aware of these caveats, however, we choose to proceed.

Structure of the book: an abridged overview

This overview not only outlines the structure of the book, it touches on all the main ideas we introduce. If you are short on time, it may be all you need to read. Then you can choose to look at specific sections for a more in-depth treatment.

Portraits of systems convening

We start with short portraits of some of the people we interviewed about their experience. The goal is to introduce them as systems conveners, give a sense of what they are trying to do as a context for their quotes, and reveal the diversity among them. They vary in terms of scope; some do very local convening in a town or a county, some act globally, and some do their work within the purview of an organization.

They also differ in the kind of challenge they take on. This diversity provides a typical sample of the countless situations that call for a systems-convening approach:

- **Complex challenges.** Organizations, governments, and the world more generally face complex problems and urgent crises that require the involvement and integration of many perspectives. Because these situations are beyond what anyone knows how to do, it is necessary to search out and include the voices of all who have something to contribute. Systems convening can leverage the know-how of experts, policymakers, as well as practitioners on the ground for addressing persistent or intractable challenges and making long-term, transformative change.

- **Innovation.** Organizational structures focused on delivery are often maladapted for innovation, which requires new connections across silos. Innovation also requires enough freedom from institutional inertia to leverage these connections and think outside the box. Accustomed to taking risks and working across boundaries, systems conveners often find themselves in a position to straddle this tension between autonomy and organizational accountability.

- **Working on a conflict.** All systems conveners have to deal with conflicts, but for some, addressing a specific, difficult conflict is the main focus of their work. High-stake conflicts demand the ability to convene all relevant parties into new forms of engagement.[1] In this book, we find cases of systems convening approaches to addressing conflicts such as interest-group negotiations in urban development, tribal allegiance in war zones, and defense of human rights.

- **Stakeholder engagement.** Many organizations have a strategic need to engage more closely with their various partners, stakeholders, and even competitors. We will see the case of a university, but it is true in all sectors. Actually, changing an institution's relationship to its environment has to go beyond outreach, increased communication, or dissemination of information that adds to the world's growing pile of unread articles and emails. The deep partnerships across boundaries that are required take skillful systems convening.

---

4 We refer here to conflict resolution in fields such as public policy and international diplomacy. It is not to detract from the important work of orchestrating conflict described by Heifetz in his work on adaptive leadership, which is something we see systems conveners doing, i.e., highlighting differences and then managing the conflict toward resolution rather than seeing it as something to be eliminated or neutralised (Heifetz et al. 2009).

- **Beyond audit.** People are recognizing the limits of traditional audits. Adversarial audits (in which an external auditor comes in and performs a list of formal checks) tend to lead to perfunctory compliance, a check-the-box and cover-my-back attitude, or even outright fabrication. Systems convening can shift audit cultures by engaging a range of players in jointly exploring the potential for real change in practice. We'll see examples in areas such as government accountability and consumer demand for more ethical and socially responsible goods and services.

- **Community development.** In local community work and in international development, there is a need to involve people directly in leading the process of developing their communities, examining their needs across constituencies, initiate projects, and undertaking the work of cultural change.

Finally, systems conveners take a variety of approaches to their convening, from opening spaces for new conversations, to running a joint project, to connecting people or promoting an idea. And most of them mix and match several of these elements.

In their voice: the work of systems convening

After introducing these systems conveners, we invite them to talk about the work they do. We present their experience along various dimensions of their work:

Crafting a convening call. From what they see as a potential, systems conveners craft a "convening call," an invitational narrative to bring people together from across the social landscape. The convening call needs to speak to people's understanding of the world and inspire them to join the convening endeavor. To work across contexts, the call is often adapted for different groups.

Earning legitimacy. Because their ability to be listened to is not guaranteed by their position, systems conveners endeavor to find enough legitimacy to work across boundaries and extend their sphere of influence. This includes building relationships and networking, as well as leveraging their own trajectory through the social landscape. Having a personal experience of various locations, perhaps by having had multiple jobs or moving from one continent to another, gives them a unique perspective on what is possible.

Engaging with boundaries. The social landscape defines all sort of boundaries, both formal and informal—including social, cultural, professional, and institutional boundaries. Systems conveners have a keen awareness of existing boundaries and of the enabling and disabling roles these boundaries play. They honor boundaries because boundaries are part of people's identities, but they are also ready to challenge them. This often entails creating and facilitating new social spaces for conversations among people who don't normally learn or work together.

Identity work. Boundaries are not just features of the social landscape, they exist in people's identities as different places they belong. Involving people in crossing and reconfiguring boundaries inevitably involves identity work.[1] Identity work, or shifting people's sense of accountability in different directions, is also key in inviting people to create a new narrative about what is possible or who they can become.

Cultivating agency. Systems conveners share an aspiration to strengthen the involvement of people often accustomed to being told what to do. They welcome bottom-up initiative. A core element of their work is to open avenues for people to have their voices heard and their perspectives taken into account. This entails new forms of capacity development that bring people together to learn from each other and discover vehicles for their agency, individually and collectively.

Dealing with power. Promoting agency often challenges the status quo. Systems conveners have to deal with established hierarchies and power—strategizing how to work with formal and informal power relationships. They develop enough political savvy to both leverage and counteract these power dynamics.

---

5 Identity work is not to be confused with the work of belonging to an identity group, although being part (or not part) of an identity group might give rise to identity work. We refer to identity work as an ongoing enterprise of being—and learning to become—a person in the world. It takes working to make sense of who you are, what decisions you make, and who you feel accountable to (or not) in multiple, changing, overlapping and contradictory circumstances, each with attendant demands and opportunities. If circumstances force you to cross a boundary or to declare or supress an identity you might be kickstarted into doing identity work. Alternatively, you might take up or fit into an identity that saves you from having to do any further identity work.

Articulating value creation. To sustain their effort over the long run and across competing agendas, systems conveners have to find ways to keep articulating the value of what they are doing to different audiences. This includes their accountability to their own organization where their work may not even be recognized.

The essence of systems convening: a theoretical model

We call them systems conveners, but most of them do not have a background in systems theory and practice. What they have in common is a certain mindset, which we articulate as a combination of four dimensions:

- They are driven by a restless determination to **make a difference** that is meaningful to all involved across boundaries and levels of scale. As a result, they are ready to take on a challenge in its full social complexity.
- They proceed from a keen awareness of the **social landscape** and its complex texture of lived practices, formal systems, and personal relationships—with the various perspectives and boundaries this entails. For them, challenges are always embedded in that landscape. Rather than bring about change from above or outside, they see the need to work the landscape from a place within it. They combine a high-level landscape view with an appreciation for the lived experience in each location in that landscape.
- They work with **people.** They place a premium on finding meaningful ways to involve people in the work. They avoid perfunctory participation but encourage people to act on their perspectives and take initiative. Developing this kind of agency while crossing boundaries is complex. It challenges existing identities. It requires commitment and the ability to navigate personal relationships and demands for accountability. It is hard work, but they see the transformative potential and they take it on.
- They adopt a **social learning** approach. Systems conveners are driven by a vision of what is possible, but they do not come to a situation with predefined answers. Rather than driving a specific change, we see them developing what we call *social learning capability*. By convening new learning partnerships, they believe that people will develop the ability to make a difference—by interacting with each other, learning about each other's perspectives, finding common ground or respecting differences. This social learning approach means that systems conveners work with people where they are and take them along on a joint learning journey.

When is systems convening the right approach?

Not all situations require a systems-convening approach. For a task that needs doing, with clear goals and objectives, a project manager would be the person for the job. If a group needs some scaffolding and enabling, call a facilitator. A broker is ideal for helping to translate ideas from one practice to another. A weaver will join the dots, strategically connecting people into new networks. An inspiring visionary with charisma is not necessarily a systems convener. Nor is a person who convenes an event or manages systems change or multi-stakeholder processes. None of these roles in themselves are systems convening, although systems conveners often play some of them and it is quite possible that a person reinterpreting one of these roles ends up adopting a systems-convening approach.

Adopting a systems-convening approach is a choice—a choice not to proceed by legislation, mandate, coercion, protest, or negotiation. It is not that systems conveners ignore systems and structures; they are fully aware of their importance and the need to address them. But their convening work starts with the experiences of the people who design or live within these systems. This is where they see the seeds of deep transformation. It is also a choice to accept the incremental nature of social learning as people explore together, often in unusual alliances, how to make progress on an issue they care about. That choice is neither obvious nor always the right one. In promoting systems convening in this book, we are not claiming that it is always the most appropriate approach. The journey can be arduous and take time. There is often pressure from stakeholders to make progress and show results rapidly. In some contexts, a systems-convening approach would be needlessly inefficient. The line between self-doubt and grandiose or unrealistic idealism can be tenuous. But for the specific challenges they are working on, systems conveners have made the bet that working the social landscape, person by person, step by step, practice by practice, relationship by relationship, will make a difference that is both deeper and more sustainable.

Leadership for the 21st century

The ability to shift your identity in changing circumstances, the artistry in dancing across historic, social, cultural, structural, or disciplinary boundaries involves work. Enabling others to do it with a sense of purpose and agency is hard. Persisting at it in organizational structures that can seem unaware or even obstructive is a feat worth celebrating. When we first wrote about systems convening in 2014, we thought it was a crucial form of leadership for the 21st century. Since then, the challenge of engaging diverse perspectives in addressing problems, being collectively prepared to deal with the unexpected, and staying agile as a way to do business, have risen in salience. It has become even more imperative to articulate better the intricate and complex work that systems conveners do, often unrecognized and unrewarded, but resolute.

2

Portraits of systems conveners

Systems Convening

Here are some examples from this book of situations that call for a systems-convening approach.

Complex challenges.
Organizations, governments, and communities face complex problems and urgent crises that require the involvement and integration of many perspectives and voices.

Innovation.
Organizational structures focused on delivery are often maladapted for innovation, which requires new connections across silos and enough freedom from institutional inertia.

Working on a conflict.
All systems conveners have to work with conflict and require the ability to convene all relevant parties into new forms of engagement to address a specific, difficult issue.

A variety of contexts

Stakeholder engagement.
Institutions must change their relationship with their environment and go beyond outreach and communication to involve the development of deep partnerships across boundaries.

Beyond audit.
Systems convening can shift audit cultures by engaging a range of players in jointly exploring the potential for real change in practice, as opposed to more traditional 'tick box' approaches.

Community development.
In local community work and international development it is vital to ensure local people lead the process of examining their needs, initiating projects and undertaking the work of change.

Let us introduce to you the people we interviewed in preparation for this book and whose experience will talk us through the kind of work they do. These are either people we already know to be systems conveners through our own networks or people we were introduced to. Some volunteered themselves. See annex 1 for the systems convening profile we shared with them in advance. We interviewed others who have influenced our thinking even though they are not quoted directly in the text; they appear in the acknowledgements.

Many people come from the field of health. This is partly to do with the nature of our connections, but it also reflects the complexity of the health system and a history of trying to deal with that complexity. Someone like Carl Davies is even recruited to "do" systems transformation. Most of them, like Madeline Hoskin and Matthew Mezey have been recruited for a job whose description they creatively interpret to include their systems convening approach.

Others come from a range of sectors from Higher Education, environmental science, and community development, to peace negotiations and human rights. Some of these people, such as Michael Fung-Kee-Fung, Neil Pakenham-Walsh and Richard Moss, are at the mature phase of an established career, and give as much energy to their convening as those who are still wetting their feet. For some, such as Caroline Rennie, systems convening is a natural fit for a life that has been rich in activism. Charles Marohn is one of the few people we interviewed who has made a name for himself as an author and podcaster about taking a systems-convening approach. A younger systems convener like Travis Tennessen, is starting to see the results of reinterpreting an established role in Higher Education to that of a systems convener. Others, like Isabel Ho, began by starting a community of practice and find themselves increasingly opening boundaries.

Conveners also work on very different levels of scale. The term systems convening may seem to connote a large scale, but many systems conveners, such as Esther Hall and Lorna Prescott, work in a local context such as a town or a village. There is all the complexity of a social landscape even at a micro level. Then there are people like Karen Tse who have ambitions for global transformations, but who work closely with local practitioners to ensure that change is realized on the ground. The scope of their landscape is shaped by their own sphere of interest and by geographic extent as well as the jurisdiction of an existing entity, such as a nation or an organization, or the source(s) of funding. Our network also led us to many systems conveners in the UK and North

America, but this is by no means a given. From Africa we interviewed Samuel Mutambo in Zambia, Pascal Djohossou in West Africa, and Rebecca Dali in Nigeria. Paula Schommer is from Brazil and Caroline Rennie from Switzerland. Geographic location did not in any way seem to determine whether or not someone takes a systems-convening approach.

**Carl Davies
Systems
transformation in
the National Health
Service, UK**

Carl used to be clinician within the UK National Health Service. At the time, he could see pervasive systemic problems and could imagine some solutions, but he was not in a position to take action.

Today, he's undertaking a PhD in how we create sustainable improvement across complex systems and works as a change agent charged with addressing complex systemic issues. In particular, policies and practices that have unintended counterproductive consequences and may suboptimize the system. Approaching his new mandates by combining his own experience as a clinician with a systems perspective, he is keen to bring to these complex challenges the perspectives of the different people from across the landscape affected by the issue. This includes relevant clinical, administrative, and patient perspectives. He gathers working groups that start by inspecting all the different perspectives on the issue, using stories to bring in the experiences of practice. This leads to a process of prioritizing the key dimensions of problems, which various subgroups can start working on.

For him, the key to solving complex problems is unlocking the agency of people who see the implications of policies in practice.

"I often say that my goal is trying to create the climate for other people and giving them the platform to solve problems they already have solutions for, but they've just never been empowered to solve."

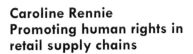

Caroline Rennie
Promoting human rights in
retail supply chains

Caroline is a Swiss consultant working for a German retailer who wants to ensure that their suppliers respect and promote human rights in their factories. The aim of their approach is to go deeper than the check boxes of traditional audits, which rarely change the reality on the ground.

Caroline's team takes a systems-convening approach. They convene local working groups in factories that include workers, managers, and sometimes owners to reflect together on specific, often difficult, human rights issues, ranging from health and safety, to living wages, to sexual harassment. Not used to working together, it takes a well-choreographed approach to get to a point where they can have deep conversations that address uncomfortable issues. Over time, by deepening relationships, the groups develop plans to bring about actual changes in policies and culture that can make a real difference to human rights in their factories.

"So I think that there is so much to be learned in … figuring out what is the minimum, what are the smallest levers that we can work with that really work to bring about a more profound shift."

Charles Marohn
Citizen groups
negotiating urban
development, USA

Charles is an American author and podcaster, who used to be an urban planner. He is the founder of "Strong Towns," a non-profit that supports

the growth of resilient cities in the US He started it out of
frustration with projects he was working on which he believed
were actively harming the places they were supposed to help.
Now he realizes that planning the future of a resilient town
requires very focused conversations with different
constituencies and groups promoting different goals. He works
with towns across the USA to facilitate multi-stakeholder
conversations about a town's future.

*"You have to ground yourself not in an economic, political narrative like
'We're going to invest in poor neighborhoods because some day it will pay
off in people earning more and having fewer healthcare costs.' These are like
propaganda math and people pick up on the propaganda math really quickly.
When we anchor in the financial conversation.What we're anchoring in is the
common struggle that every local community has, which is 'We have to make
the budget work.' And you can be left of center, you can be right of center, you
can be a centralizing person, a localizing person, it doesn't matter.Wherever
you are, you have to make the budget work…And so we anchor it in the
common math and not the propaganda math."*

Esther Hall
Public health as a
community concern,
UK

       Esther is trying to transform a small town
in the north of England. She works as a Systems and Strategic
Change Specialist in Public Health.She is currently helping to
decentralize public health as part of a move by the National
Health Service to bring decision-making to local authorities.
A large portion of their current funding comes from Sport
England with a view to expanding the influence of physical
activity in public health. Her team is piloting a process by
which public health can move from a centralized concern of
experts to a joint concern of citizens and local authorities. They
convene groups and conversations to help citizens find their
voice and power to shape their own lives and their health.

Esther works with a team in a local community; they work to develop meaningful connections between people in ways that allow them to take up the initiative and make small, relevant changes to their life.

"You try to really pull people in that space of different perspectives ... In the beginning I thought I could sit in a cupboard and design something, even if we added to it later. When the team came, I realized that I had to leave that behind. Don't start designing until the team is in place. And give them time to sit and absorb it all. All the communication around money really clouded the way people saw it. It takes time."

Isabel Ho
Community of practice
on patient risk
management, UK

Isabel is a Therapeutic Radiographer working in the UK and she has been convening an interprofessional community of practice on quality and safety for radiation oncology. The community has now grown national and has started to organize a conference. It is aiming to be the place to go for people in all related disciplines to improve the practice of quality and safety in radiation oncology.

"We are a very specialized discipline. It is not easy to break the boundary to work with others in other disciplines even though we share similar challenges."

Karen Tse
Ensuring legal
representations for all
accused worldwide

Karen is a former public defender from the US. She was the Supervising Attorney for the Cambodian Defenders Project, and was a Judicial

36

Mentor for the United Nations Center for Human Rights in Cambodia. She has now dedicated her life to ensure that every person accused of a crime around the world has access to legal representation. As well as being an international human rights attorney she is also an ordained Unitarian Universalist minister.

The non-profit she founded in 2000, International Bridges to Justice, is focused on the provision of early access to a lawyer for the accused. They are building local communities across legal professions, law-enforcement, and government in over 100 countries to develop the practice and identity of "justice maker" among the various players involved in the delivery of justice, from police officers all the way to ministers of justice. She works both bottom-up and top-down supporting on-the-ground defense lawyers and involves as partners the police, prosecutors, and judges who may be perpetrators of human rights abuses and are often seen by some as "the enemy."

"We want to know 'What are your deeper values? Why did you become a police officer? We think you want the country to move forward. Who are you and who do you want to become? Where do you want to go? How can we co-create a future together?'"

Lorna Prescott
Developing a local culture
of curiosity, creativity, and
connection, UK

Lorna has been working for many years in the town of Dudley in the UK testing experimental social infrastructure. The goal is to catalyse regenerative cultures through hands-on practical and creative projects designed together by residents of the town. Her team is convening all sorts of networks and groups to encourage citizens to co-create a place in which people can thrive. Their social lab includes a physical space where people can congregate and start new initiatives. The idea is to shift systems by legitimising and cultivating many small experiments and activities led by local people, and bringing them into relationship with each other, by changing the initial conditions—working to build the social soil that nourishes them.

"Our ultimate goal is resilient, regenerative places which everyone can have a hand in creating."

Madeline Hoskin
A systems-convening approach to project management, UK

Madeline is a programme manager in the UK National Health Service. Rather than starting with the traditional project plan, she starts by convening all the relevant voices, engages them with the issue, sees what emerges as they start working differently together, and moves forward with actions, and then in retrospect, rationalizes what is left to be done in terms of a clear project plan.

"I'm always torn in two. That pretty much describes the act of doing this job... I have a foot in two camps—one foot in now and one in the future. One in the practical and another in the strategic at the same time. That balance and managing that tipping point is where I sit... I feel like I am making serendipity happen."

Matthew Kálmán Mezey
Network for improving health and quality in healthcare, UK

A former journalist, Matthew is in a Communications team in a healthcare foundation, working in partnership with the National Health Service in the UK. He convenes a heterogeneous online community of around 4,000+ people trying to improve the quality of healthcare. He is constantly pushing the edges of this community so that a greater diversity of voices can be included and at the same time, constantly connecting people across contexts who may benefit from interacting. Even outside this community he can't help but connect the dots and finds himself creating multiple holding spaces for conversations—and action—that can make a difference.

> *"I like to think I've got all these little bits of possibility that I've parked there, and I can see them. And eventually you see things lining up and you quickly put them back into play."*

Michael Fung-Kee-Fung
Regional interprofessional approach to improving cancer care, Canada

Michael is a clinician and professor of gynecologic oncology at the university hospital in Ottawa, Canada. He uses his legitimacy as a respected practitioner and organizational leader to convene regional, cross-organizational, interprofessional communities of practice that take on joint leadership in improving care for various types of cancer, from diagnosis to full treatment. He also works at national and international levels to spread this approach.

The key to Michael's convening work is to get all the groups involved to agree on the nature of the problem and then to accept that they own part of the problem and part of the solution. For him, an authentic understanding of the problem allows practitioners to see their own perspective truly reflected in the group's take on the issue. This allows people to share ownership of the problem, to step out of their organizational roles enough to commit to contributing to a genuine solution rather than pointing fingers or defending turf. While initiated by the urgency of specific cross-silo problems, many communities have continued. Sufficiently outside of organizational structures to anchor innovation in honest reflection on practice across boundaries, these communities now constitute the creative "backbone" of a health transformation agenda for the region.

"My experience extends because I have a lot of people beyond me, who are driving their own convening. It's a ripple effect. I have a layer of people who are authentic in different areas who are driving this independently as well. It's not orchestrated. I may be a subliminal architect, but it's really driven by their authenticity."

Neil Pakenham-Walsh
International community of practice on health information systems, UK

Neil is a British medical doctor who is now fully dedicated to convening an international community (HIFA.org) that promotes a world where every person has access to reliable healthcare information and is protected from misinformation. Functioning mostly online, the community explores healthcare information needs and how to meet them. It has a focus on low- and middle-income countries and collaborates closely with WHO. People from almost every country in the world belong to the community, over half of whom are front line health workers, while others are publishers, librarians, researchers, social scientists, and public health professionals. The community operates in four languages — English, French, Portuguese, and Spanish.

"It had been a failure of communication among the various stakeholders. I was surprised that they weren't actively convening people across health information systems. ... There is no one who has stood back and looked at where the system is dysfunctional. Always focused on one component of the problem."

Pascal Djohossou
Community-led development in West Africa

Pascal is the Regional Director of The Movement for Community-led Development in West Africa, who works on mobilization for sustainable development. He has moved away from the more traditional approach of managing projects for development to framing the bringing together of people with different perspectives to help them discover what values in common are driving them at a deeper level.

"A long time was focused on how to manage projects. We need to frame it differently. We mobilize by focusing on intangible resources, on fundamental values, not just projects. Governments and Civil Society Organizations and other stakeholders have different notions of sustainable development, but common fundamental values are driven by what people value at a deep level."

Paula Schommer
Improving government transparency and accountability via cross-boundary engagement

Paula is a professor of public administration at the state university of Santa Catarina in Brazil. She works to increase transparency and accountability in local government. She also belongs to several transdisciplinary groups related to her discipline, often working in partnership with ex-students who come to them when they need help in improving public services and accountability systems.

She convenes working groups consisting of local bureaucrats, politicians, civil society organizations, and oversight agency auditors to develop new, more collaborative ways to improve the functioning of local government and to co-produce public services. She finds that these conversations help break down stereotypes that different people have of each other.

"Everybody knows that we are not being able to solve this problem, despite having all the conditions. So the problem is about how we connect all the conditions we already have in terms of knowledge, of power, information."

Rebecca Dali
Tribal conflict
resolution in Nigeria

Rebecca is a Nigerian peace activist who set up the Center for Caring, Empowerment, and Peace Initiatives. One of her initiatives has been to bring women together across religious and tribal boundaries to address lethal conflicts. By developing trust through sharing their experience as women, the group found a new strength and devised ways to convince men to stop the killing. Through the organization she set up she also works to reintegrate women who have been kidnapped by Boko Haram and who are rejected by their families and communities when they return. Forced to leave the country, she received the UN Sergio Vieira de Mello Award, which is an award aimed at drawing attention to the unnoticed efforts of individuals and groups who are "doing something special and unique to reconcile people and parties in conflict." Over 350 babies have been named after her as gestures of gratitude from mothers she has helped.

"I started my research on the effects of violent conflicts on Christian and Muslim women. I started following them. The way I empathized with them was to share my story. 'We are all in this together' because I've been there before."

**Richard Moss
How to use science
productively for local
action on climate
change**

Richard is a US climate scientist who worries
that the numerous models and predictions produced by
various scientific disciplines related to climate change are not easy for
local decision-makers to use for their practical purposes. Richard wants
to transform the way science is used to make climate-related decisions
at the local level.

He and his colleagues have been convening the Science for Climate
Action Network to bring together into thematic communities of
practice local practitioners, technical assistance professionals, as well as
scientists from related disciplines in the natural and social sciences. The
goal of the communities is to use sustained learning interactions among
these constituencies to produce guidance on how to make scientific
models and predictions relevant and usable for local decisions.

*"The thing that's scary to me as I look at the moment that we're in in the
United States, we have a new administration coming in that's articulating
wonderfully ambitious goals, essential goals. We have to achieve them. ... But
I worry that the administration is going to take a top-down approach, that
under the pressure to get going straight away, they will feel the need to just
tell people what to do. My experience has been that implementation is not most
effective with that approach because it doesn't pay attention to the very
different barriers that exist to implementation in different places and the
types of capacity that you have to build in order to overcome those barriers.
And that's a much more nuanced thing, which is why we believe this sort of
sustained approach to assessment is so important."*

Samuel Mutambo
Community-led
development in
Zambia

Samuel manages community-led development rural projects. He is the coordinator for the Movement for Community-led Development — Zambia Chapter. He became disillusioned with traditional development projects that he thought more often than not left communities poorer than before the project started. He advocates for a development that is local and community-led for the purpose of sustainability and self-reliance.

He works by bringing local stakeholders together to take charge of their development projects. He always involves local communities and traditional leaders in leading their own development with the aim of achieving self-reliance. Government structures are also involved to ensure that everyone speaks the same language and understands how a project they devise will benefit each of them.

"How to help people become self-reliant? How to enable people to take ownership over the process of their development? ... When communities are mobilized, they know who they are and what they need, and they can start envisaging their future prospects together. We have two development issues: community-led development at the community level and the movement for community-led development organized at the national level. We are creating a single platform for civil society organizations, government officials, academics, and individual activists. How do we get all communities to feel that they are talking with one voice at community and national level?"

Travis Tennessen
Building a deeper
connection between
higher-ed
institutions and local
communities

Travis was hired by Western Washington University in the USA to lead the community learning program. Typically, people in this position act as brokers between the community and the faculty to help find placements for students to have learning opportunities in the community. But Travis started to take a systems-convening approach to the task.

Travis created a program called the Community Engagement Fellows, which was initially a professional development program for faculty, not only at his institution, but from the four higher-ed institutions that served the same community. Over time, Travis started to invite more and more leaders from non-profits and government in the community as well as higher-ed faculty and staff. Together the diverse group explores projects that can be developed across the higher-ed campuses and the community. People bring their challenges and proposals to the group and the members act as learning partners to work on these challenges and brainstorm ideas and solutions. This ongoing community of practice is forging deep bonds between the local higher-ed institutions and the community that go well beyond the traditional community-learning placements. People are getting to know and trust each other and finding all sorts of ways community groups and higher-ed can collaborate.

This approach is now being recognized and adopted by other institutions, first in the state of Washington, but now in other states, and even in other countries. Travis is building a network of institutions learning with each other how to convene Community Engagement Fellows programs. The shared learning includes how to account for the value of university–community engagement beyond the traditional metrics of hours of student community service. It is a matter of understanding how community engagement changes how place-based higher-ed institutions function to live up to the motto of the program: "Learning as if the real world exists."

"I learned to say explicitly …that we were bringing Higher Ed and non-profits together, that we were bringing these different campuses together because we were all serving the same community. People wanted a space to do that."

What these portraits reveal is not only the variety of contexts in which systems conveners operate, but also the variety of approaches they adopt to do their work, sometimes exclusively but more often in combination.

- **Hosts of an encounter.** Many host encounters between people who usually do not interact, talk to each other, collaborate, or see each other as potential partners. In hosting these encounters, systems conveners strive to give participants insights into each other's practices, goals, and perspectives, and to discover new ways they could work together.

- **Custodians of a social learning space.** Some go further and act as custodians of enduring spaces for ongoing cross-boundary learning. This is different from hosting boundary encounters in that it requires a sustained commitment and participation by a regular group over time. Many conveners are cultivating heterogeneous communities of practice to bring the perspectives of different constituencies to bear on an issue and help them develop their respective practices in orientation to each other. They seek a delicate balance between the integrity of the space and the need to involve a greater set of voices in the process.

- **Project initiators.** Some systems conveners initiate projects that allow people to cross boundaries by collaborating on achieving a joint outcome.

- **Advocates.** Some people like Charles Marohn are advocates for an idea or an approach they are trying to promote to enable people to learn and work together across boundaries.

  Connectors. Systems conveners often make connections between people who are related by an issue, but who may not know about each other or have a way to work together.

What all the systems conveners we talked with seem to have in common is a deep, almost irresistible, urge to make things work better in the landscape in which they find themselves. Many of them are have been influenced by an ideology or religion they have encountered on their journey. All are driven, persistent, and manage to be both willful and pragmatic at the same time. Few, if any, do it for an extrinsic reward and few seek recognition except as a way to be able to continue their work. In forming relationships, they generally put their own reputation on the line to build and leverage networks and to invite people into the value of doing things differently. Their passion can be absolute, and many find it hard to hold back. Their formal job description rarely recognizes the time and care that goes into achieving small but significant results. Layered on top of conventional activities and deliverables, this can easily lead to burn out.

Now that we know something about them, we can listen to their own voices to understand better the work they do.

3

In their own voice:

the work of systems convening

Systems convening is not merely a vision or a sense of possible connections; it is work. While the work is complex and diverse, it is useful to articulate a few key dimensions to make sense of what this work is. The dimensions of work we describe here take different levels of salience at different times and are often tightly woven together. But if we are going to help systems conveners become more articulate about what they do, have it recognized, and find guidance for it, it is useful to see these dimensions of their work as requiring different strands of intentionality.

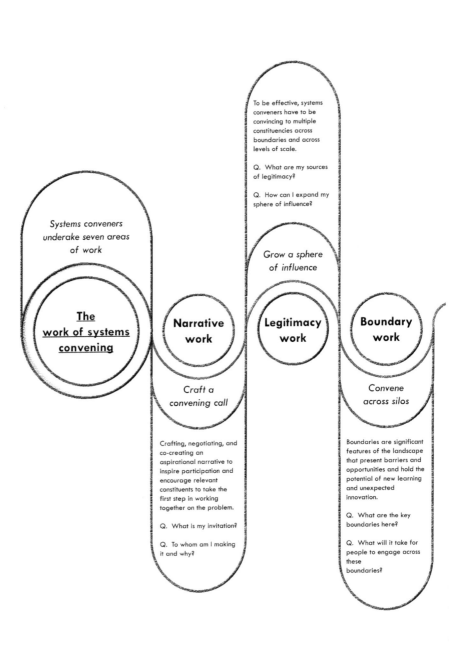

Systems conveners underake seven areas of work

The work of systems convening

Narrative work

Craft a convening call

Crafting, negotiating, and co-creating an aspirational narrative to inspire participation and encourage relevant constituents to take the first step in working together on the problem.

Q. What is my invitation?

Q. To whom am I making it and why?

To be effective, systems conveners have to be convincing to multiple constituencies across boundaries and across levels of scale.

Q. What are my sources of legitimacy?

Q. How can I expand my sphere of influence?

Grow a sphere of influence

Legitimacy work

Boundary work

Convene across silos

Boundaries are significant features of the landscape that present barriers and opportunities and hold the potential of new learning and unexpected innovation.

Q. What are the key boundaries here?

Q. What will it take for people to engage across these boundaries?

Working in a complex landscape can require you to develop the ability to identify with multiple places in the landscape at once.

Q. What are the sources of identity?

Q. How is my intervention challenging people's sense of identity?

Q. What new identities am I inviting people into?

The social landscape is shaped by power structures: institutions, hierarchies, practices, groups, historically defined categories of people, and even individual trajectories.

Q. How can we enlist the support of existing power structures?

Q. What established power structures might be challenged?

Support personal transformation

Deal with power structures

Identity work

Agency work

Power work

Narrative work

Cultivate the power to act

Articulate the value

A core role is to unlock the capacity that already exists in the system, drawing on the experience of practice as a deep source of wisdom.

Q. What kind of convening will allow people to discover their power?

Q. Who is not empowered to act on their understanding?

The initial narrative work needs to continue in order to articulate the results of the work, both within organisational reporting lines as well as across the wider system.

Q. What difference are we making?

Q. What is the potential change and for whom?

Narrative work: crafting a convening call

> *If our accountability is for the wait time for treating patients, well,*
> *that's not a surgeon's problem only—that's a hospital problem, a*
> *surgeon's problem, a radiology problem, a biopsy problem, etc. There's*
> *about 10 people involved in that problem. So now people have to share*
> *the ownership of the accountability problem.*
> — Michael Fung-Kee-Fung

Like all systems conveners, Michael is crafting a "convening call." It is an aspirational narrative about the potential he sees for approaching a complex problem in a collaborative way. It is a call to action, an invitation for relevant constituents to take the first step in working together on the problem. To the extent that people can see their experience and perspective in his call, it acts as an invitation into convening work.

As an aspirational narrative of action, a convening call can include a goal, but it is more than a goal. It is a description of what is happening and a generative description of what could be happening. It is a narrative that sets the stage, potentially guides action, and provides an interpretive framework. Thus, Michael even builds into his convening call a transformative promise that will engage participants beyond the immediate problem that brings them together.

> *We invite people to solve a problem they believe in, but it's part of a*
> *wider transformation of redesigning and reinventing how we deliver*
> *health care. ... You do have to have a bit of a transformative*
> *dimension to your issue you are dealing with. So yes, we're trying to*
> *solve flow and lead time for lung cancer patients, but really, we're*
> *trying to solve the death rate from lung cancer. You have to have*
> *something a little higher up, so that the group having had some initial*
> *success would want to go back to that thing again and chip away.*
> — Michael Fung-Kee-Fung

A convening call does not have to be the same for all stakeholders. In fact, in most cases it isn't. A convening call can be more or less flexible and adapted to different constituencies. Some conveners have multiple different calls. For example, Carl Davies talks about the role that control plays in constraining change, and the power imbalance that often prevents those who have the answers from delivering solutions. This awareness leads him to craft two different calls for his convening work in the National Health Service—one for the "controlled" and one for the "controllers." For those he calls the controlled, the practitioners and the clinicians, the call is fairly straightforward.

> *Look, here's your opportunity to do the kind of things you've been wanting to do for a while and I'm going to help create the climate to enable you to do that. So, I need your ideas, I need you to engage with this work and in return I'll help tackle those things that have historically constrained you.*
> — Carl Davies

For managers and policy folks at a senior level, it takes more work to convince them to become involved because it is harder for them to think of relinquishing control.

> *My call to the contracts and policy teams was very different and required an awful lot more and very different work to try and win their trust than it did the other part of the pathway ... and it's an ongoing piece of work to get them to shift, fundamentally, the way we approach things and start to build what we do far more on trust and collaboration. than on policy and contractual management and control.*
> — Carl Davies

A convening call has to balance personal inspiration with the web of accountabilities people live with. So, a convening call can build on people's sense of commitment to their organization as well as a chance to improve themselves and to do their own work better.

> *...learning how to do your work in the place you're in, and keep your eyes out to what people are doing in other communities, and have relationships beyond... People want to feel like they're participating in something cool, and something important, and [that] they're a Fellow.*
> —Travis Tennessen

Here the convening call directly appeals to participants' sense of the importance of a mission and how it can serve their own purpose. There is a lot of variety. Some calls focus more on the individual and some on the collective. Some are pragmatic (e.g., a problem to be solved) and some idealistic (e.g., a longing for justice). Some emphasize the urgency of a current state of affairs (e.g., a costly conflict), while others emphasize the long-term benefits of collective action (e.g., preparing for upcoming climate change). All convening calls reflect the convener's understanding of the landscape and of what will resonate in various locations. This can lead to a very prosaic invitation.

> *We don't tell people we're doing deep culture change. We ask them*
> *what needs repairing in their house.*
> — Lorna Prescott

The intention here is not to mislead, but to find a meaningful entry point for people to become involved. It has to resonate with them: they have to see themselves and what they care about. There is a subtle art to crafting a convening call that resonates. It has to be solid enough to inspire, but open enough that it can be appropriated and reworked by the people who respond to it.

> *I understand that I can't go in and frame things in a logical way.*
> *People make decisions based on emotions and relationships. It's great to*
> *frame things, but you have to make that really human. All the facts in*
> *the world won't change anything.*
> — Charles Marohn

Part of the process is creating a picture of what is possible that propels people into collective action, so that once they get going, they discover possibilities for themselves.

> "In reality, it's very hard to get a community to do something if no one
> else has done it, even if they know it's good. They have to see others
> doing it. No one wants to be the first. You have to put a spin on it —
> talk about the good things they are doing, even if it's not
> journalistically balanced … You have to create the avatar of an
> accumulation. You have to create a narrative of progress, even if it's
> spotty. … You smooth out the edges and make this thing seem maybe
> more than it is. … So, you could say: If you want to do this, you can
> go through two years of in-fighting and all hate each other and come

*out with something that's not as great as you envisioned. Or you can
say, This is where they were, and this is where they ended up. Isn't
this great? And you can do this too. ... And what you essentially do
is build a narrative of success because the next people to go down
that path will have fewer obstacles and they will have learned from
someone else doing it. And they will probably reach further than that
last one or reach beyond what they were able to do.*
— Charles Marohn

The notion of a convening call may make it sound like it is an explicit, ready-made narrative that reflects a clear and articulate vision. Sometimes, it is, but the reality is usually more tentative, negotiated, and evolving than that.

I had to sing the song before knowing the words.
— Esther Hall

Over time, the convening call will evolve as new voices become included. It is refined and expanded to become a collective product. A convening call is an invitation to others to contribute their perspectives.

*My funder once asked me, "Well, what's the vision?" I said, "I'm not
going to tell you what my vision is because that has to be something
that is contested, collaborated on. It will be ever-changing and
ever-growing." So right early on in the project I refused to answer that
because I'm creating the conditions for a collective vision to emerge.*
— Lorna Prescott

A good convening call often reflects a personal awareness of what brings people together at a deep level. It speaks to people's hopes and open avenues for action.

*There is a lot of naming and shaming [of people involved in human
rights abuses]. My sense was that even if you name and shame, you
have to go beyond that. You have to create new possibilities... There
is a huge world of opportunity. Lots of laws on the books about early
access to a lawyer are not being implemented.*
— Karen Tse

Legitimacy work: growing a sphere of influence

A convening call only works to the extent that the convener has enough legitimacy to be listened to. When working across a landscape and across boundaries, legitimacy is not a given. It doesn't come encapsulated in a tidy job title. It is not guaranteed by one's position or qualification. In order to be effective, systems conveners have to be convincing to multiple constituencies across boundaries and across levels of scale. Some conveners do have the official legitimacy of a mandate or role through their organization, but even these conveners still have to work to sustain that legitimacy and translate it into action.

> *My initial mandate gave me a level of legitimacy and gave me the*
> *opportunity. That opens the door for you and then you've got to stay*
> *in the room. And I think the first part was opening the door and*
> *we had this platform to build those relationships and trust but that*
> *would have very quickly fallen down if I wasn't able to keep people*
> *engaged with the kind of approach I was taking, the language I was*
> *using, and the relationships I was building. I think my legitimacy has*
> *almost come from really starting to back up the kind of things we were*
> *talking about and starting to demonstrate the benefit of working in a*
> *very different way.*
> — Carl Davies

Even when the initial legitimacy starts with a reputation or institutional qualification, it ultimately depends on a genuine connection with people and enough understanding of the landscape that conveners can reflect the perspectives of various constituents.

> *I would say the first part was based on shared salesmanship or selling*
> *of an idea. I'm a little bit grey in the hair ... so I guess at some point*
> *you become embedded in the woodwork. But I don't want to create any*
> *illusion that what we do is easy or is successful all the time. I don't*
> *want to create any such illusion. ... A lot depends on the authentic*
> *articulation of the issue you are trying to bring forth. I use the word*
> *authentic because a lot of the initial acceptance has to do with the*
> *person who brings it up or starts the conversation, actually has an*
> *authentic interest in what they are bringing up. Things that are driven*

primarily by organizational quid pro quo endeavors are a little less
exciting. It's things that are driven by people who see it as a genuine
problem.
— Michael Fung-Kee-Fung

A persistent commitment to making a difference becomes a robust source of legitimacy over time.

How I have gone about cultivating legitimacy? I think it is mostly a
blend: being an officer of an organization which has a long history
and is well respected in Dudley, having worked in local neighborhoods
for over 20 years now, and bringing stuff to life—influencing by
doing, making things happen, not just talking about it.
— Lorna Prescott

A history with a domain and with the people involved can also be a source of legitimacy through continuity. A university setting, for instance, gives both intellectual legitimacy and a history of working with alumni as they take positions in relevant organizations.

I really study the topics, the field, I'm really engaged in research and
keeping in conversations with people from inside and outside the state,
the country. It's a way... we try to be updated about the debates,
internationally, nationally and locally—to be in contact with the
people who are really working in the field. ... We have been working
with these topics for a long time, 7–8 years now. And continuity. We
have new people arriving to these positions, but I already know the
story, the people who worked before you.
— Paula Schommer

In the absence of an institutional history of working together, legitimacy can also come from raw reputation in the world.

I feel like the legitimacy comes, has grown, in a sense, based on the
size of the crowd. I can now turn to the people in our audience and
say, "You're not a fringe group of people." The things you believe, the
things you are working on is not something that is fringe. It might

*have been true ten years ago, but at this point there's a couple of
million people reading our stuff.We do an online meeting, and a
thousand people show up. We put something online, and it reaches tens
of thousands of people.You're not alone and you're not crazy, there's
a whole bunch of people buying into the same conversation. They're
doing amazing things.You can do amazing things.*

*In a sense the numbers give you more legitimacy than expertise. That
may be wrong morally ... having more followers doesn't make you
more right, it doesn't make you more correct or morally a better person
but... I can walk into a room where I talk to people and I don't have
to explain who I am for them to listen to me. I'm with Strong Towns
and that's enough legitimacy to be invited into the conversation.*
— Charles Marohn

Honesty and transparency are key to the trust necessary for the development of
legitimacy.

*One of the ways that you get legitimacy, I think, is also building trust.
So, what we've come to is that actually in our very first discussions, we
acknowledge what brings us there, and then we say, since the program
is happening, how can we make it worthwhile for all of us. This can of
course be something where you are trying to check boxes. Right? But
we're not trying to check boxes.We are trying to see what's actually
happening, with you, in a way that together, everybody who is involved
in the system under discussion can be a part of finding solutions to it,
and helping those solutions spread. So, it takes a while to build that
kind of trust, and on the whole, we have a reputation for that trust.*
— Caroline Rennie

This includes being transparent about what is not known, or not certain,
especially in contexts that straddle research and practice.

*I talk about these limitations, these doubts, these obstacles.We talk very
openly about the difficulties, the answers we don't have.*
— Paula Schommer

At ground level, a lot of legitimacy is simply based on personal relationships.

> *Building relationships with individuals is a way of sowing seeds for the future.*
> — Isabel Ho

Careful listening is therefore a key component of gaining legitimacy.

> *... once they can see that I am just with them, I am not an arse, you know, I am listening. I am really listening. I think they can see; I hope they can see, I think, the heart. There is no dressing up. There is no dressing up of this. This is the reason. This is why I am asking this of you. It's only so that this can be better. If that is really what you are thinking, or what you are feeling on the ground, then you let me know. It is very collaborative.*
> — Esther Hall

Some systems conveners work the landscape as a way to build relationships through a process of establishing legitimacy one person at a time.

> *What I primarily relied on was having those coffee dates and building that rapport with people so they could think of how to go back to their organization that this was a good use of their time. And I gave them enough examples. I'd tell them about good things that came out of it for people like them. "Oh yeah, so this other librarian was involved last year—do you know her?" "Oh yeah." "Well she's got this interesting lecture series going now because she was involved." Just to give people some sense of how they could tell the story of why this was worth their time ... It wasn't just that they were liking me, because my personality didn't have to be central to that. They liked what I saw in them and saw why what they were doing is important. Just saying something like "you have something good to offer."*
> — Travis Tennessen

For this kind of "retail" legitimacy, systems conveners need to leverage their own history, identity, and experience. This can depend on personal characteristics that make connections easier.

> *It's harder to be a convener if you don't have... I mean, I have a lot of benefits. I have a PhD. I'm a straight white man ... so, I could go into a professor's office and we could talk about our dissertations and about classes that we teach and have all of that resonance in an instant. And a lot of people in offices like mine don't have that background and that identity, so becoming a convener is not as easy as for someone like me.*
> — Travis Tennessen

For someone in a different position, legitimacy is likely to be harder. A lot more persistence is required until one gets accepted.

> *I'm thinking in the early days it was more difficult because I was more junior, and you are poking your nose. There were many meetings where basically they said, "shut up, we don't care"... but I think developing these relationships and kind of connecting, and often just helping. Just always say, yeah, is there anything I can do? You are having a bit of trouble? Is this something I can help with? Is there a workshop I can do? You are just constantly offering help. And not asking for anything in return. That's it. No expectation.*
> — Esther Hall

When connections are not easily established, working with a local team can be a useful source of legitimacy.

> *In the community? Well, it's more difficult because it becomes less about all of that and more about, do you come from here? Does your family come from here? How do you talk? It's more that stuff, so I really have less legitimacy with the community themselves. ... So, my legitimacy on the ground is through the team rather than directly with the community, I would say.*
> — Esther Hall

Still, many conveners are working in the cracks, reinterpreting their job to include systems convening, but without the organizational legitimacy of a job title to be doing what they do. Systems convening is not something that our current organizational and societal structures can easily recognize and support. Most systems conveners end up having to work, at least to some extent, under the radar. They artfully make a difference by bypassing the usual channels, pragmatically demonstrating their accountability to the places that matter, and persisting in their efforts to work the landscape at a deeper level. While most of them would probably wish to be recognized by the organization, their driving passion is to bring about a fundamental change in ways that they think matters, sometimes without much consideration for the cost to themselves.

"I do a lot of systems convening as part of my online community man-agement work. But it remains mostly invisible because it does not fit in the usual boxes. That does not stop me because it's important to do. But in terms of upward career path, it's not clear how it can help."
— Matthew Mezey

Boundary work: convening across silos

From a systems-convening standpoint, boundaries are significant features of the landscape that present both obstacles and opportunities. They are challenges, but they also hold the potential of new learning and unexpected innovation.

"It's about bringing together lots of people's truths." — Esther Hall

Conveners inevitably have to confront traditional and enduring boundaries. There are boundaries of practices between people from different backgrounds or professions. There are boundaries of commitment with accountability to different goals or outcomes. Organizations create boundaries of affiliation. Hierarchies and levels of scale create boundaries between people who have power over each other or have very different access to resources. National and cultural boundaries reflect different historical contexts. Categories of identity also create boundaries that can be difficult to overcome, as can tribal affiliations. Across boundaries, people often see the world differently, have different perspectives on what matters, misunderstand each other, see people as "other," dig in their heels or reach out, become cynical or hopeful, try to destroy or become curious, engage or disengage.

And some of these oversight institutions said no, we don't work with politicians, we can't work with local members of the parliament. This is a political problem, and we don't want to be part of something that can be used politically.
— Paula Schommer

Across boundaries, people are often biased by stereotypes and blame each other for long-standing problems.

> *And this is one of the key things I want to be able to do development stuff and the unconscious bias stuff in there, because that's the key bits of what we are challenging, not challenging, trying to help people move past. It's exactly that because as soon as we got there, it's, you know, oh it's them young people. They are the trouble. Oh no, it's them old people. They are the trouble. No, it's these incomers, now, that's what, you know, everyone's got a version of who it is.*
> — Esther Hall

Operating across a social landscape, systems conveners see engaging at boundaries as central to their work. But they are not iconoclasts. As they work with different types of boundaries, they navigate a paradox. On the one hand, they acknowledge existing boundaries as inherent in the very nature of the social landscape—the unavoidable result of the social, historical, political, and institutional structuring of the human world. Boundaries are neither good nor bad—just a fact of life. And conveners respect how people experience or value boundaries as part of their identities and their view of the world.[1] On the other hand, they are ready to push, reconfigure, cross, or even break down boundaries when they stand in the way of what they are trying to do. So, opening up a boundary is a balancing act between the integrity of the spaces people have created and the welcoming of new voices.

> *I'm pushing the edges without falling out. ... I'm always trying to change the boundary so it doesn't become exclusive...You have to make sure things are loose enough that people feel like they can do something alongside the official members.*
> — Matthew Mezey

---

6 Boundary work, a term attributed to sociologist Thomas F. Gieryn was used in the '80s and '90s to describe boundaries between science and nonscience. It started as a way to explain how scientists maintain the boundaries of their community against threats to its integrity (from, say, fraud and pseudo-science). The term was then found useful to study the demarcation between the scientific and the political in advisory relationship between scientists and regulatory agencies. This latter work (such as by Jasanoff 1990) suggested that blurring the boundaries between science and politics rather than separating them can lead to more productive policy making.

When people get comfortable in a familiar space, opening it up to new voices always involves taking a risk.

> *We are opening the door. We don't know how far we can go ... We need to embrace whatever comes when opening the door. We might find another door we need to open up. We have to embrace the unknown.*
> — Isabel Ho

In order to solve the kinds of complex problems systems conveners take on, they have to get people to engage across boundaries. While recognizing that boundaries can be highly problematic, systems conveners don't treat them as facts to accept or reject, but as learning opportunities.

> *And I have all the people in the room and what was really interesting is that in isolation when you have those conversations, even when you reflect back to them that perhaps what they're seeing isn't how it's being seen elsewhere in the system, they can defend their position one on one. But whereas once you got everyone in the room, they were saying "Oh I didn't realize that. I was totally ..." Whatever their position was at the time, they are far more open to change and understanding. And I think it's that kind of slow process of drip feeding the problem and then getting everyone in a kind of safe space to discuss it so we establish a shared understanding of the problems we face as a system.*
> — Carl Davies

Personal stories are a good way to get people to appreciate each other's experience.

> *Stories were really important. The first piece of work was to connect with the people who actually have to deal with the results of the policy and capture those stories, so that was what we did. We went through all the steps of the system, captured examples and stories of how it was having a negative impact on patients or clinicians. And then we framed it in this meeting as a way, in non-threatening terms, of saying: well actually for the most part, the policy works really well and has a really good purpose, but actually there are some unintended consequences of that, and these are what they look like for patients and for clinicians and for management. And*

actually, some small tweaks to what we do might well give us a more sophisticated set of solutions.
— Carl Davies

Charles Marohn takes it one step further by always reframing the problem in a way that allows all sides to start the conversation without feeling they have to promote or defend a pre-established position.

We start to engage in a common struggle around "We have to make the budget work"... In all the complexity, finance is the lynchpin. ...We start with the financial question. That brings everyone to the table. Then, rather than talking about financial constraints we talk about 'What are the tradeoffs?' We bring different groups to the table allowing people to build off of that, with us as the anchor. We change the conversation to one of "We can do that, and these are the tradeoffs."
— Charles Marohn

In some cases, it is important to create a shared artifact, something that acts a "boundary object," around which cross-boundary conversations can be organized.

There is the mapping, like I said, which is, we often have people walk about in a factory, in small teams of two or three. And then say, where in that factory is it dangerous to be a woman? Or, where in this factory is it dangerous to whatever the issue is. And then when people come back, all these pieces of paper show up, with the areas that are dangerous, and why. And it's actually eye-opening. So even if a manager has not been there, for most of the day, in that moment, if you can bring them in and they look at that and they go, I had never thought about that. ... it's a shock to them, this is news. They did not have it before. That can generate a shift, an internal shift where they can no longer unknow that.
— Caroline Rennie

For some systems conveners, producing boundary objects that can serve to mediate a boundary is a convening call. The community of local practitioners, technical specialists, and scientists that Robert is convening around climate change is producing boundary objects to help guide the use of climate-change science for local policy and decision-making.

And it got to the point where I had done multiple rounds of these assessments, (the kind of thing I described early on that's report-based), and I had also had enough conversations with people at an implementation scale ... to see that the assessments weren't as useful as they could be. ... And so, it just seems to me that it's really important given that the next multiple decades are going to be about implementing climate policy, whether it's for emissions or for resilience, that we have to get a system that's better for applying, for providing useful information.We have a lot of people working at the local level.We have people working at the national scale. And we have people working in scientific fields. But we're missing this middle-ware, this meta-knowledge of how to apply this in use cases that have some similar characteristics...I see it as an urgent need and one that without it, people without information about climate change are going to take a lot of actions that may not be effective.
—— Robert Moss

In Robert's community, the process of producing boundary objects starts by listening to local practitioners describe the decisions they need to make in order to prepare municipalities for coming changes, such as managing wildfires or increased flooding or incorporating climate risks in economic planning. Then working groups inspect the various models and predictions produced by science, reflect on the usefulness of different methods for different types of situations, and produce joint guidelines. This type of boundary work is delicate because the subtleties of various practices can easily be missed across boundaries.

[Climate change] is one where you really do need a crystal ball, but there is no crystal ball. So science is the substitute. And if we don't do science in a way that recognizes uncertainties and how people can still use information that's uncertain. And if we pretend it's certain, if we're not careful how we describe the bounds of certainty, then people are going to make real mistakes that could have consequences for livelihoods and lives. It's that which makes me committed to this.
—— Robert Moss

Before people can engage seriously across a difficult boundary, however, it is often necessary to prepare the ground by getting them to see each other as fundamentally human, beyond roles or stereotypes, just as people, who can be partners in a new conversation.

We work a lot with empathy. So, for example, in discrimination, we'll say, think of a time when you were harassed or discriminated against. And people write a whole story. And then they fold it up. And they put all these little folded pieces of paper in a jar. And the jar gets shaken around. And then it gets passed around and everybody picks one out. So now nobody knows who is reading whose. Right? And everybody will stand up and read what they have. And what you realize is that the human experience of having been harassed or discriminating against is universal. And in the moment, the people feel that. And then you can add on to that, you know, what dreams do you hold for your children. And you realize that the dreams are also quite universal. ... And that creates a space and a room in a discussion that you can then, you can start to move with that and start to work with that, in ways that help you think about, and how else could things be?
— Caroline Rennie

In some extreme cases, boundary work can be difficult because people may be locked in positions, not just by their own beliefs, but by the stances held by constituencies they are accountable to. We talked about boundary work with a diplomat (who has to remain anonymous). For her, the key to crossing boundaries in very delicate, political situations where lives are at stake, is to create a safe space, secretive and walled from the outside world in which people are freed from immediate accountability to positions strongly held by their home base. There, they can engage with the boundary and explore new perspectives and possibilities, which in the best scenarios, may end up reconfiguring the way the boundary is understood and addressed. Only then are they ready to discuss this in a more public forum.

Identity work: personal transformation

Boundaries are generally tied up in people's identity. Working with boundaries thus entails working with identities. It goes without saying that moving beyond a personal boundary and trying on a new identity that might be in tension with your evolving self can be hard. It is a behavioral change that takes time. And if someone is fearful about expanding their identity, they can dig in their heels. It can take some nudging and coaxing for people to look beyond their personal horizon, whether it is someone entrenched in their role in an organization, or a young adult ensconced in a PlayStation.

*Before some can be active [in community health groups] you have to
get them to look up from their PlayStation. The question is what's the
next step beyond your PlayStation? One step at a time. ... I am this
guy that sits on a sofa for 12 hours a day, playing my PlayStation.
That's who I am. .... Just getting them to ask, what do I want? What
might I do that's a bit different than this?—or not! It might be
... am I, you know, someone who might change my sock choice? Buy
a funny tie? I don't know. Something! It's simple little bits of just
flicking them slightly outside the ordinary.*
— Esther Hall

Living in a complex landscape entails not merely expanding your identity or even
inhabiting a new one; it means being able to modulate your identification and
identify with multiple places in the landscape at once.

*You have to multi-identify. You do have to give up something. You have
to give up the fact that working across a silo is not possible. You have
to accept the fact that although I'm an oncologist, I really have a lot
to learn from my radiologist. Although I'm a clinician, an adminis-
trator, I have to learn a lot from finance and the business world. You
have to give up your silo. That's your disidentification. Fundamentally,
you have to re-identify as a multi-dimensional human being, which
you are naturally, which is the liberation component. We go to school
and we are wired down into a box because that's how the corporate box
can best match you. You're a yellow, you go in yellow. You're a red, you
go in red. The whole world is convening where it doesn't matter what
color you are, if tomorrow you want to be red and tomorrow you want
to be yellow, it's cool.*
— Michael Fung-Kee-Fung

Some systems conveners see identity work as the very essence of their convening
and its transformative aspirations. They see convening as calling upon new
identities that will inspire people to engage in new partnerships to make a
difference.

*We want to know about your deeper values. "Why did you become a
police officer? Who are you and who do you want to become? Where do
you want to go? Can we co-create a future together." It's about reaching the dignity and worth of every person, not just about surfacing*

corruption. ... It's also true of the powerful people. We are looking for the good in each person. Whatever sector, there are always some people who want to transform themselves and their country, people who do want peace and justice. It's about creating identity. It's about finding an identity for people who are not defenders, like police officers. We have to get them to think "I am a defender. I am a justice maker." We need to help them become part of the community that transforms the justice system.

— Karen Tse

Some conveners even anchor their entire convening work in a shared identity as a way to transcend a boundary. This is particularly effective when the convening call reflects the convener's own identity. In the story below, Rebecca Dali's invitation resonated in large part because of her own identity as a woman who had lost a son to the conflict.

In that area, my friend called me and said, "We have to go to that community." I said, "Let us call the women." We got some funds and called for Muslim and Christian women. We agreed not to use abusive language, that we are all women, more compassionate than men. We're here because we love everyone. We're here to sympathize with each other. They shared their story about how they had been treated. The Muslim shared their stories of how Christian men with guns killed people. Christians shared their own story too. We comforted them. I shared my own story about losing my son. At the end of the meeting, they came to understand that they are all sufferers, and they are all survivors, and they are all victims. And they didn't know what they were going to do with their men. We called another meeting at a different spot. By now, we have all become friends: no more quarrelling and looking at each other. They were hugging each other, saying: "We have to tell our men to stop. We don't want them to continue with the war." Together, they found new strength. They devised some strategies to convince the men to stop the killing. And in 2004, that conflict stopped in the whole community, for more than 1 million people. In more than 20 local communities, they stopped.

— Rebecca Dali

Agency work: the power to act

Top-down policies and organizational demands for compliance often end up
keeping people from acting on what they know. A common conviction among
systems conveners is that the experience of practice is a deep source of wisdom,
but that silos and defined roles limit the ability of this wisdom to engage with
complex problems.

> *When I was in clinical work, I could see the answer, but I did not have
> the power to act on it. From my experience I'm not alone on that, I
> think as communities of practice we all know the answers, but
> indiviually we are often constrained within the boundaries placed
> upon us by organizational structures.*
> — Carl Davies

Engaging across boundaries is a way to expand this wisdom, give it a voice, and
put it to good use. The new partnerships that emerge from this engagement
allow people to discover the power to act on what they know and find
meaningful ways to make a difference, individually and collectively. For many
systems conveners, especially those who share Carl's background in the
experience of practice, opening up agency is the deeper transformation that
drives the more visible work they do.

> *Yes. I think that's the sole focus of what drives me... that we funda-
> mentally change the way we operate as actors within the system. I hope
> that would be a lasting effect. It's not so much about the work, it's
> about the approach to what we do and who we are and how we connect
> across the systems. So, I expect that that is the case and I certainly
> hope that what I'm trying to do is show people there is a different way
> to work; and still get either just as good, if not much better than we've
> historically gotten. And I would hope that the people around me, and
> I feel that I get that back generally, that it's been a positive change
> for them. And we've all learned an awful lot about the way we can do
> things differently as we move forward together.*
> — Carl Davies

Many systems conveners see their role, not so much to create agency where it is missing as to unlock the capacity that already exists in the system. It is reaching the point where people can act on what they know.

> For me it's all about liberating capacity. It's all about liberating the abilities of people, systems and teams to do X. ... So, people need to have agency. And I think it's agency about their learning. I think it's their agency about the ability to impact. A lot of people have to learn that, if I connect with a manager and she and I work on something, or I connect with three people in this system, we can do something...
> People like working with people who are trying to do something.
> — Michael Fung-Kee-Fung

And for some systems conveners relying on people's agency may be the most effective way to make things happen when you don't have authority over them.

> It is all about building up that agency. But it's not out of any will-fulness; it's out of the structural position I'm in. I'm in a position, essentially of not having loads of people I can tell what to do. So the only way I can do lots of stuff is through their own agency. I have to sort of lure them into being more themselves.
> — Matthew Mezey

If the goal is to create the conditions for collective agency based on what people really value, then setting the tone is a key aspect of the work of systems convening.

> First, we need to talk with people about what they value. The way you move through the village is fundamental; it's crucial. What is the best leader at the village level? Not someone who knows everything. It's someone who is humble and open. It's someone who says, "I don't know everything, but we can build something together." ... If you come as a teacher, people are very polite. They'll say, "Thank you. We were expecting such a teacher for a long time." But if you come in openly and say, "We can build something together," things can move from there.
> — Pascal Djohossou

Once the tone is set, people will feel that this is not business as usual and seize the chance to join in doing something they find meaningful.

And it really gives them all the power. All I am doing is bringing the roof frame—and they are really bringing the rest. ... I think through that kind of approach and a real respect for them, and the community, I think, all of these things together, they can feel it.
— Esther Hall

But agency is not a concept or an idea. It has to be experienced in practice to become real. Creating the conditions for agency can require some convening discipline.

It's not about aid, it's about solidarity. [A person from] the group who started to do craft together, and right at the early stage she came to me and she said, "Surely you've got some money in your budget that we can buy some resources. Some of these people don't have any money." And I said, "Well, that's not how we're doing this work. We've got the space for you to use. Can you not reach out in your networks, on social media, and we can do the same and see what craft resources people might be able to donate or that already exist." ...A few months later she came to me and she said, "You were right. This group is now sustaining for much longer."
— Lorna Prescott

Systems conveners only feel that they succeed if they manage to convene the right partnerships for people to continue the process themselves.

I'm freeing people from that myth ...We have more agency, more capacity than we give ourselves credit for. ... It's core to what we are trying to do.... If our work doesn't result in local communities recognizing that they have the capacity to do things themselves, for themselves, then we are failing. We are not doing our job.
— Charles Marohn

Creating the conditions for agency sounds good in theory, but in practice, it is a delicate task. Agency is not merely an individual characteristic, not even a collective one. Rather it is inextricably woven in the broader social fabric. Changing agency changes established relationships, both for those who gain agency and for those who interact with them. This has profound implications for identity. For instance, increasing the agency of workers shifts the identities of managers from someone who makes decisions and gives orders to someone who listens and engages with people to address issues.

> It is something that I brought into the program a lot because I think that it's vital, particularly for managers, that they understand their identity. Because with workers we are automatically doing that. We are talking about agency. We are working with them in a way that gives them agency. We are asking them for ideas, we are asking them for questions, we are asking them for proposals, we are asking them for assessments. So, they are used to that now. They are getting used to doing some of the work. But for managers, if the factory starts running on its own, then, what's their role? And I think that that's the question, that's what we need to hold, which is what does it mean to be a good manager if your factory is running itself?
> — Caroline Rennie

Power work: dealing with power structures

Opening up agency, however, opens up all sorts of issues of power. The social landscape is shaped by power structures: institutions, hierarchies, practices, groups, historically defined categories of people, and even individual trajectories. Power plays are ongoing, subtle or obvious, hidden or in full view. Different power structures create a significant dynamic in the work of systems conveners, as most end up challenging the status quo. By threatening existing power structures, systems convening can give rise to agendas that militate against the ability to convene. But even success can be thwarted by attempts to appropriate what convening has achieved for different ends. Systems conveners thus need to be politically savvy. They need to learn to both leverage and resist existing power structures.

> Shifts are destructive. You can't do a shift without destroying relation-ships ... When you start to really push a shift or change, there will be opposing forces building up against you. Not because they have an anti-you agenda, but those who didn't have a stake in the game now do. Knowing this early on can help you mitigate.
> — Anonymous

Power can sometimes be wielded unwittingly, appearing simply as business as usual, but undermining the empowerment work that a systems convener has been working on. Resistance does not necessarily come from high places and those who stand to lose from power shifts are not necessarily people with the most power. It can be those in the middle.

> We thought the community would want to be empowered. But there
> are bits of the community in positions of power (like people sitting on
> Boards) who are not interested in being empowered, but in playing out
> the game they learned to play. It's that band of power in the communi-
> ty that stops things from moving forward. ... It's like the community
> is kind of bubbling through with its own solutions and its own way of
> doing stuff ... That's coming through, and then the local authority
> comes in with "This is how you do it." ... So, it kind of squashes it.
> — Esther Hall

In addition, in a role that requires networking and leveraging personal influences it is almost inevitable that systems conveners will bump against gender or other systemic power issues.

> It sounds awful, but it is a bit of an old-boys network. It definitely is.
> Resigning yourself, myself, that's what it is. and trying to work round
> it. ... But at the same time not, because by playing the game, you
> become the game.
> — Esther Hall

It is important to be able to name these power structures as a way to start resisting or shifting them.

> A recent conversation I had with someone who was convening another
> neighborhood and he asked for some help with facilitation. I asked
> who he was bringing round his table. And when he said some of the
> names I said, "my observation would be that some of the people you
> are inviting are older white men who have huge amounts of positional
> power and experience of leveraging money and getting a slice of the
> pie that you're putting on this table and there are people who are

always missing out."He heard me. He didn't do much about it. But I felt confident to say to him as one of those men, this is what I'm seeing. There's something about being able to point to who gets to wield power.
— Lorna Prescott

The work of systems convening usually takes place in organizational contexts—directly or indirectly. These organizations, even those with a commitment to transformation, are often still structured primarily around delivery processes, with bureaucratic procedures and top-down accountability that are in tension with the need to be adaptive. This makes it important to involve people from higher levels who have the authority to deal with this tension.

We have great support now from so many people and so many administrators and we have stood the test of time. ... So, part of the magic is that you have to get the top to enable the bottom. If we don't have the top, it's an exercise in futility, like the charge of the light brigade. So, part of your convening is that you have to convene the top as well. You just can't be ... you work in organizations. The world delivers all of our services within organizations. They are not bad. They are just not dynamic enough to liberate people and to adjust to things in a quick way, which is not what they were designed to. But it doesn't mean you throw them out. It means you create capacity within them to maneuver them. It's an evolution of organizations to be honest.
— Michael Fung-Kee-Fung

The more iterative and incrementalistic approach of systems conveners—seizing the moment, thinking out of the box, quickly discarding what doesn't work, and building on what does—can be anathema to an organization that relies on rules and procedures for its smooth functioning.

For something that is so essential as we become more adaptive and fluid, it's hard to stay in the background. And there's a danger, a danger it can be destroyed. Because it is a beautiful thing. It doesn't take much to destabilize. One manager from a different background can destabilize. It's fragile but powerful.
— Madeline Hoskin

Even when systems convening is oriented to organizational challenges, its innovation capability needs to operate outside the formal organization. This requires a balancing act: keeping close enough to the organization to have support and influence but separate enough from the organization that the convened groups remain free to explore and innovate on their terms. In this sense, systems convening is similar to the work of serial entrepreneurs.

> *All the work we've ever done wasn't sanctioned officially until it became a head of steam that became sanctioned and built into the system. It's almost like you're building a start-up and it gets accepted into the system and you give it over and it becomes part of the system. And then you build another start up and you just keep infiltrating the system.*
> — Michael Fung-Kee-Fung

In many contexts, the success of a convening endeavor completely depends on leveraging existing power structures.

> *People can't work together unless they agree. Most important is to understand who we are and what we intend to do. Also ensure that government officials understand the objectives, how it will benefit the government and how it will benefit the community. If you fail to let the government understand, it's difficult to get the buy in.*
> — Samuel Mutambo

Even when power structures are a threat or the direct cause of problems, it can be essential to engage directly with those in positions of power. They too may discover new ways of thinking by crossing boundaries, and a change in them can have far-reaching consequences.

> *If we are doing a training for human rights people, it's very important to invite the Minister of Justice to your training. Some people think of them as the enemy—but we do not. One of our defenders was picked up and probably tortured. But it's important to find that part of the identity of the person who has the power to make a change.*
> — Karen Tse

Narrative work: articulating the value

The narrative work of systems conveners starts with the convening call, through which they invite people to join their convening efforts. But this narrative work needs to continue as a way to articulate the ongoing value created by systems convening. There are many reasons for this. First the work of systems convening is often hard to pinpoint, to systems conveners themselves, let alone other stakeholders.

> *I sometimes think—what have I done all day? It's hard to describe things that are intangible, but I know the outcome wouldn't have happened without doing all those intangible things. ... Sometimes it feels painful. You get the great joy of something you have connected turn into something beautiful. You know it wouldn't have happened if you hadn't brought it together. But nobody knows.*
> — Madeline Hoskin

Indeed, the most important parts of the work remain largely invisible. Systems conveners have to be true to their understanding of their work and the meaningfulness of their own aspirations while addressing the expectations of their organization or funders.

> *Much of the work that's done that makes it successful is the spaces and cracks in between. It's the invisible plan and energy that makes it all come together. ... So much that moves is intangible. But funders want something very specific. You have to say the breaks and lunches are longer.*
> — Karen Tse

People working in different departments, institutions, or silos have to deliver results along their own lines of accountability, regardless of their commitment to the transformation in the new configuration. Thus, systems conveners have to be responsive to multiple agendas and can find themselves struggling to demonstrate value on multiple different fronts. This calls for highlighting the importance of cross-boundary engagement where previous attempts to solve a problem haven't worked.

> *It's being able to resolve issues that have been long-standing around contracts and finance and new ways of working. I think that's what builds legitimacy and provides value, once you can show evidence that you have been impacting things that haven't been resolved using the old approach.*
> —— Carl Davies

Ideally, over time, participants start taking it upon themselves to tell stories about the value they are getting.

> *And over time as people have learned about the program, not from me but by someone else who participated, then they have already got the value-creation story from that person, which is so much better than from me.*
> ——Travis Tennessen

It can be useful to help frame this process. Actually, the participant's manual put out by Travis's team includes a simple template for telling stories of value creation.[1] Working in local community development, Lorna Prescott goes one step further and invites members of groups to become what she calls "detectorists"—members who actively search out and articulate the value they are creating by learning together. The team has designed a scrapbook for people taking on this task.

> *Someone who is passionate about learning to crochet or something can become part of a group of people who are doing this thing together. And they're getting all the benefits we get as humans when we're connected, learning skills, and sharing things. Some of those people, not all of them, are drawn through to the deeper narrative by our introduction to the idea that through our work we invite everyone to be "detectorists." We say that's about using the secret powers we all have to come together to learn. [Then the questions for detectorists are:]*

---

1 This template is based on the value-creation framework that we have developed to articulate the value created by social learning in communities of practice and other social learning spaces. This framework distinguishes eight types of value created by social learning and provides a format for structuring "value-creation stories" about how social learning ends up making a difference (Wenger-Trayner and Wenger-Trayner, 2020).

> *What's changing because we're doing these things? What's different?*
> *What's possible? So, some of the people who have been involved in*
> *hands-on projects either undertake their own participant observations*
> *and reflections. And / or they join learning sessions maybe around their*
> *project or a set of projects. And our researcher leads conversations.*
> *She's very adept at drawing out much bigger themes.*
> — Lorna Prescott

Deep change through convening takes time and commitment to connect across boundaries.

> *In the early 1990s nobody was actively convening people across the*
> *global healthcare information system. I saw this as a key weakness of*
> *the system and an opportunity to make a difference. It's got a lot big-*
> *ger, and we are continuously expanding our membership and linking*
> *with other organizations. I don't see my role as very different to how it*
> *was then, but when I started, I didn't realize it was going to be such a*
> *long and gradual process.*
> — Neil Pakenham-Walsh

This makes it all the more important to be finely tuned to where value is being created, to monitor and document it systematically, and tell stories about it, where possible. It will develop the sense of empowerment that people gain by knowing that they are having an impact.

> *How do you keep the narrative going? In my organization, what I do*
> *is not very mainstream, but the way we keep the narrative going is that*
> *you do have to keep the main theme of the conversation true, which*
> *is working across boundaries, learning together, and you bring this*
> *camaraderie around the joy of the quest — in many ways, by learning*
> *together, success together, [achieving] something together.*
> — Michael Fung-Kee-Fung

Slipping back into the familiar is easier than maintaining a new way of doing things. Systems conveners need to help people see the value of engaging across boundaries as a way of sustaining a new identity.

> *As with any kind of behavior change you can always relapse and go back to the old way of doing things. It's probably one of my interests in complex systems is that kind of natural entropy—how systems naturally decay over time. But if we shift it so far … that gives us enough to produce some really good outcomes, and actually embed some of those behaviors. The longer those people can stay connected to the approach and continue to see the benefit I think we're more likely to see a behavioral change in them as well as what happens across the system.*
> —— Carl Davies

Institutional expectations usually emphasize short-term results, often in the form of easily tracked indicators. But complex work that involves changing identities and cultural norms is longterm. It is more likely to be reflected in ongoing series of micro-shifts rather than in sudden, dramatic impact. Given the fundamentally incrementalistic nature of their true impact, systems conveners need to play the long game.

> *And everybody wants to get a quick win, to get the "golden egg out of the goose" as quick as we can. But really you have to play the long game. And the reason to play the long game is because it's too painful to do multiple short games and somehow people have to get to that place. But the communities of practice we had way back then still exist. They are now the backbone in our region for a whole health transformation ecosystem agenda.*
> —— Michael Fung-Kee-Fung

4

The essence of systems convening:

a more theoretical look

Systems Convening

The mindset of a systems convener has four dimensions

Restlessness to make a difference

A determination that leads them to embrace challenges in their full complexity and requires navigating between opposites.

Social landscape perspective

A deep awareness of the social texture of the human world, in terms of systems, practices, and relationships defined at multiple levels of scale.

Commitment to identity work

An engagement with people as meaning-making agents in the landscape, whose identities are key to reconfiguring the landscape.

Social learning approach

Approaching a challenge or an aspiration by developing the ability of people to learn from and with each other how to make a difference that matters to them.

There is a common foundation to the way systems conveners understand the world and their work in it. Just as foresters, runners, or biologists each have their own way of looking at a landscape and might notice different things about a scenery, systems conveners share a specific way of looking at the social world. Explicitly or implicitly, when striving to make a difference, they tend to look at challenges and opportunities in similar ways. We have distilled this perspective as a combination of four dimensions:

- **A restlessness to make a difference:** a determination that leads them to embrace challenges in their full complexity and requires navigating between opposites
- **A social landscape perspective:** a deep awareness of the social texture of the human world, in terms of systems, practices, and relationships defined at multiple levels of scale
- **A commitment to identity work:** an engagement with people as meaning-making agents in the landscape, whose identities are key to reconfiguring the landscape
- **A social learning approach:** approaching a challenge or an aspiration by developing the ability of people to learn from and with each other how to make a difference that matters to them

This section is our interpretation of what systems conveners do and it is informed by our perspective as social learning theorists. Our hope is that articulating their approach here in the language of social learning theory will contribute some useful perspective to their work.

A restlessness to make a difference

A key characteristic of the systems conveners we have encountered is a restless determination to make a difference that matters. This is, to us, the quintessence of the spirit of systems convening. Such determination to make a difference in practice has important consequences for their work and their experience of it.

The first and foremost consequence is that they cannot bring themselves to simplify a problem to make it amenable to a quick solution. Their stance and approach to all aspects of their work reflect this insistence on achieving results that are meaningful to all while taking challenges in their full social complexity. Because of this willingness to do what it takes, they seem to learn to manage tensions between what often looks like opposite ends of a spectrum. These tensions arise in their relationship with their environment as well as the personal attitudes and skills they bring to their convening:

In their relationship with their environment

The work of systems convening is always directly or indirectly contingent on institutional contexts and expectations, but it is not something that is easily recognized and supported in current organizational and societal structures. Because their entrepreneurial spirit does not simply follow established norms, because they will not reduce their aspirations to merely fulfill compliance with formal expectations, because they insist on judging for themselves what needs to happen, systems conveners can easily be seen as mavericks in their organizations. Yet they are not—overtly or at heart—troublemakers: they strategically learn to make the system work for their convening approach to making a difference.

Bridging closeness to the ground and political savvy. When seeking the power to make a difference, systems conveners are usually not at the top of the relevant decision- and policy-making hierarchies. Operating closer to the ground allows them to be better connected to the realities of practice and the attendant communities and networks of influence.[1] But it means that they must also be strategic about connecting with the powers that be when formal authority is needed to get things done.

Navigating the trade-offs of visibility and invisibility. Most systems conveners feel that the nature and value of their work remain largely invisible—they are aware of the lack of recognition, support, and career prospects this entails. While they would probably welcome being better recognized by their organization, their driving passion is to make a difference in ways that they think matters whether or not it fits in existing schemes; many end up having to work, at least to some extent, under the radar. Some degree of invisibility has its advantages. They are prepared to bend rules and situations to serve their end, when compliance comes in the way. Innovativeness often requires operating outside the immediate scrutiny of established organizational demands. They artfully work toward the difference they are trying to make by navigating or even bypassing the usual channels while pragmatically demonstrating their accountability where they need to.

---

1 These connections to key networks has been called the "network secret of change agents" (Battilana and Casciaro, 2013).

Juggling short term and long term. Systems conveners have to balance long-term visions and aspirations with short-term demands and opportunities. Getting buy-in from different stakeholders, crossing boundaries, and finding alignment all take time. However, keeping stakeholders happy and participants engaged often requires producing short-term results and looking for low-hanging fruit. Conveners need to keep the long game in mind while taking advantage of every opportunity that presents itself. This largely incremental, iterative, and improvisational approach—seizing the moment, quickly discarding what doesn't work, and building on what does—can be anathema to an organization that has relied on rules, procedures, advanced planning, and well-defined targets for its smooth functioning.

In being a systems convener

To fully embrace the subtleties of their work, systems conveners need to display seemingly opposing dispositions, attitudes, and skills—without descending into a split personality.

Passionate and pragmatic. They are on a personal mission they feel passionate about. The motivations and emotions that drive them are always strong, even if they are varied: hope, disappointment, authenticity, anger, wisdom, vision, spiritual quest. They are frequently personally pained, sometimes as a result of their own experience, by the unrealized potential they see in the world around them. At the same time, they have to be pragmatic about how to achieve their goal. They do not let their dedication and zeal come in the way of getting things done. They deal at once in poetry and prose.

Willful and inviting. Their determination to make a difference pushes conveners to be uncompromising in driving their endeavor. But their vision of the possible is an opening rather than a closing. Ready to engage with the social complexity of a challenge, they frame their aspirations as an invitation rather than a directive. Seeing that other perspectives, components, and dimensions are needed requires that they be ready to relinquish control, which is hard when you really believe in what you are doing and when you want to make sure your efforts achieve the difference you see can be made. And while their aspirations are ambitious, conveners need to frame them in achievable steps that make sense to the people they hope to involve. They have to combine planning and opportunism, managing and schmoozing, forcefulness and negotiation. They tend to be all at once highly social, well networked, attentive listeners, good communicators—and curiously alone.

Big-picture driven and detail oriented. True to the wide-angle lens they cast on the nature of a challenge, systems conveners live in the big picture. It is the wellspring of their passion. But they are also aware that the devil is in the details. An eagle-eyed attention to details is especially important for the little things that make people feel welcome and invited to take part. We have often been awed by the ease with which a big-picture thinker can move to talking with great care about the placements of tables in a room or the hues of a background color.

Impatient and persevering. Systems conveners usually feel a sense of urgency. They want to see things moving. But their project is long term, and they take some risk by exploring paths not taken. They need to persist through the inevitable failures and setbacks. Remaining upbeat is crucial to keep people inspired, but it demands resilience: setbacks can only be bumps on the way. Often, changing course to adapt to new circumstances and involving new people is the way to continue moving in the same direction.

Being all these things at once may be too much to expect of one person. To increase the likelihood of covering all sides of these tensions, many conveners work as a team. Either way, the restlessness to make a difference entails embracing inherent tensions and navigating them artfully. People who are good at this kind of work seem to excel at holding contradictory exigences at the same time, rather than trying to simplify life by resolving the tension one way or another.

A social landscape perspective

In order to make the difference they care to make by taking on the full social complexity of their challenge, systems conveners proceed from a tacit or explicit awareness of the complex social, cultural, and political texture of the social landscape in which they live. They pay attention to the different entities, boundaries, relationships, identities, cultures, and power dynamics that constitute that landscape.

Structuring elements

The various entities that constitute the landscape are not just the formally recognized ones. We focus on by three interrelated types of structuring forces that configure the landscape:

- **Systems:** sets of designed elements, institutions, projects, activity structures, and artifacts that shape the landscape
- **Practices:** what people actually do and the competences and approaches they have developed to do what they do[1]
- **Relationships:** people or groups of people who are bound by commitments, friendships, similar experiences, labels, or other ties

For instance, an organization consists of an institutional structure as a designed system, with its stated goals, units, roles, jobs, procedures, rules, and hierarchies. It is also constituted by the practices that the people who live in this institutional design have developed to contribute to, comply with, or to resist the system. And it is also shaped by interpersonal relationships among people.

Systems, practices, and relationships all create boundaries, loyalties, and power dynamics, but they are distinct. There is a constant interplay among them, but it is not a deterministic relation. Practices may or may not be aligned with the relevant systems. In practice, systems may or may not give rise to the effects intended by their designers. And the effects of relationships on systems and practices are difficult to predict. Systems conveners are as concerned with what happens in practice and relationships as they are with the systems that were designed to structure them. They have to work with all three to achieve sustainable results, without romanticizing or demonizing any of them. Working with relationships and including the voice of practice as well as influencing the design of systems is often why convening is central to a convener's efforts.

Levels of scale

Systems, practices, and relationships can exist at all levels of scale, from the very local to the global, and everything in-between. Each level of scale is its own landscape, with its own complex set of systems, practices, and relationships creating entities, boundaries, and power structures. Levels of scale also create boundaries. And each level requires its own systems convening work: no level simply subsumes another; convening work at one level does not obviate work at another; something working at one level of scale does not imply that it will work at another. Systems are often used to achieve scale. There is a price to scaling: you lose some of the texture of relationships and how things work in practice.

---

1 This distinction is similar to Jürgen Habermas's distinction between the lifeworld and its colonization by instrumental systems, but here we do not associate instrumental intentions with systems only or assume that practices are free of instrumental thinking/actions.

Including the perspectives of practice and relationships makes things more complicated. In a social landscape, scale is not free.

Systems, practices, and relationships are in interplay in constituting the landscape, but they don't necessarily exist at the same level of scale. Very often they do not. For instance, a companywide policy will affect the local practice of a unit. Conversely, a globally defined practice like a specialized type of surgery will be done in the institutional context of a local hospital. Many problems are exacerbated, rather than solved, by a mismatch of scale between systems, practices, and relationships. Because systems conveners operate in the interplay among all three, the multi-scale nature of the landscape is crucial to their work. Very often, involving more than one level of scale is a dimension of the problem and of the solution. Different stakeholders are invested at different levels of scale. They often blame other levels for enduring dysfunctions. Whenever a challenge includes multiple levels of scale, convening work need to cross these levels. At whatever level of scale systems conveners primarily act, they must deal with the interactions, influence, interdependencies, and power relations across different levels of scale. This does not necessarily mean that conveners always work at multiple levels of scale at once, although in many cases they do. But they have a finely-tuned awareness that at any one level of scale, there is a range of other scales likely to need working.

Landscape as metaphor

The metaphor of a landscape connotes something fairly concrete that people live in and travel through, noticing, adapting to, and shaping its geography. It conveys a complex texture of contours and boundaries, relationships and power structures, entities and viewpoints. Mountains and cities convey the idea that certain areas are already occupied by practices and systems, communities and institutions, relationships and influences—with all the opportunities and challenges this historical configuration presents.

A landscape has both natural and designed features, raw material and built systems. A landscape is not static, but neither is it easy to change. It can be refashioned and reconfigured, but not without challenging the established, being prepared to take advantage of unexpected opportunities, and preparing for resistance. The social landscape is an artifact, a product of history. As designed elements, systems are both the creations of certain practices and given life by the relationships and practices they shape. The landscape does not sustain itself; that takes ongoing work.

Working the landscape

Systems conveners work the landscape from the inside. They live in the landscape like everyone else. They cannot stand outside or do their work from a detached perch. They acknowledge, and often leverage, their own location in the landscape as well as their specific trajectory through it. Many of them are travelers, across practices, systems, relationships, and levels of scale: they have personally experienced many locations, metaphorically speaking. Most conveners we speak to have crossed personally challenging boundaries—across countries, cultures, disciplines, religions, organizations. Traveling gives you a unique perspective, which you would not have in any single location. You build a resilience to the bumps and knocks. It allows you to see patterns others do not see. It encourages a certain optimism about the unknown and your ability to take advantage of the unexpected. And it confers you some measure of legitimacy when talking with people.

We all develop a picture of the world that helps us make sense of who we are and what we do. For systems conveners, in particular, a deep sense of the texture of their landscape is a foundation for their work—whether they call it a landscape, an organization, the context, or the system. Developing this kind of cross-boundary "knowledgeability" is different from developing competence or expertise in a specific area. It involves developing an orientation to practices in which one cannot claim competence, with enough understanding to see how those practices fit in the overall scheme of things. Knowledgeability in this sense is key to the ability of systems conveners to interact productively across the landscape.[1]

In the diversity of locations, patterns, and dynamics in the social landscape, conveners cannot help but see connections and opportunities to do something that will make a difference. When they see the potential to do something, systems conveners see that challenge, not only as an issue in and of itself, not even as an issue for one practice or one system, but in terms of its concrete embeddedness in a social landscape. How do systems, practices, and relationships at various levels of scale shape what happens? Who are the players involved? What are their various perspectives? What can they learn by coming together? What boundaries exist? What comes in the way? Where is a potential missed? Where are there opportunities to create new connections?

---

1 With the focus on communities of practice, learning can be theorized in terms of the regime of competence of specific communities. When theorizing learning in a landscape of practice, we introduced the concept of knowledgeability into our social learning theory to expand the social perspective on learning beyond the confines of specific communities of practice (Wenger-Trayner and Wenger-Trayner, 2014).

Mapping the landscape

When we work with systems conveners, we usually start by drawing a rough map of their landscape. We use a set of icons to depict various elements such as institutions, projects, communities, networks, as well as individual players. We use different colors to show scale, and lines and arrows to show the direction and depth of connections. We always ask the conveners to put themselves in the map. Often, we also ask them to draw what they perceive as their sphere of influence. We have done this exercise in a room on big piece of butcher paper or online using a collaborative software.

The point is not to get the map just right, but to engage in a reflection on the structure of the landscape, who lives where, who does what, what relationships are relevant, and what accountabilities exist that will influence the work. The emerging picture can become quite messy, but systems conveners always seem to find the picture and the conversations about it useful in articulating how the challenge is embedded in the landscape and what they are trying to do. The map helps build their awareness that any issue is not experienced in the same way across the landscape. They use it to understand where there are opportunities and barriers, and where some social spaces can be opened to start new conversations. Most importantly, they use their grasp of the landscape to talk to people in ways that reflect an understanding of these people, their situations, their challenges, and what they could conceive as a potential way forward.

A landscape perspective is not without its risks. The complexity of so many connections can seem overwhelming. Seeing the big picture and talking about the landscape can feel like an achievement in itself. In a reflective moment in an interview, one convener even mused half-jokingly that taking the landscape perspective and trying to make connections that lead to something could result in a god complex. The point for systems conveners is to translate seeing connections and patterns into real convening work; it doesn't stop at understanding or creating a vision.

A commitment to identity work

Ensuring the broad meaningfulness of an endeavor entails working with people. The landscape is not an abstract concept; it is populated by people. And people are complicated. As crucial as it is, working the landscape in terms of systems, practices, and relationships at multiple levels of scale is only half of the stance of systems conveners. The other half is readiness to work with people: it is a commitment to the human experience, a commitment to convening people as full human beings, with complex identities, including their history, aspirations, perspectives, and competences, but also their disappointments, diffidence, cynicism, and conflicting loyalties.

A key part of understanding and changing the landscape is to develop an understanding of people's identification within that landscape. The focus on identity starts with the convening call. Without formal authority, working the landscape cannot be a top-down restructuring. Participants have to identify enough with the convening call to make it their own. The prospect of a reconfigured landscape has to offer them new ways of seeing and experiencing themselves in that landscape. Unable to see people as cogs in a wheel, systems conveners seek to nurture agency because it is a critical factor to create identification with their endeavors. If the drive is just an interesting idea or a perfunctory going along, it will be superficial and short-lived, as too many such activities are when they are not guided by a convening heart. Engaged identities are key to a commitment to sustainable change.

Systems convening almost inevitably sets up the conditions for people to do some identity work. Not that people are likely to call it identity work; it is more likely to be an experience of readjustment or even pain as someone finds they have to adjust their behavior to be accepted or listened to on the other side of a boundary. This is hard work. It is personal. It touches people's core. Reconfiguring a boundary can create new in-group commonalities and out-group distinctions, change who is in and who is out. Engaging across a boundary can be threatening to one's sense of self. Existing identities may not function well, and people can feel vulnerable when what counts as knowledge, competence, or power doesn't have the same currency as it does on their own side of the boundary. It is one key reason systems convening can meet with resistance. Whenever reconfiguring a landscape involves shifting boundaries, enabling and resisting forces will arise. This requires a fine understanding of power relations and counterpower moves. But it is always a person who experiences power, whether wielding it or being subject to it. It takes identity work to have the right power dynamics in place. Identity work is at the core of systems convening— understanding who people are and helping them see themselves differently.

A social learning view: identity as work

Understanding the nature of identity from a learning perspective can inform the work of systems conveners. Social learning theory closely associates learning and identity: they are dimensions of each other. In this view, identity is not a given; it not a thing that exists in and of itself. It is not a role or a label, even when these contribute to shaping it. Rather it is an experiential process: the ongoing work of being a person, over time and in relation to a complex and dynamic social landscape.

Identification and dis-identification. Identity work involves processes of both identification and dis-identification. We identify with certain elements of our landscape and we dis-identify with others. We include certain associations in who we are, and we exclude others. Sometimes identification and dis-identification are a choice, driven by aspirations or resistance; but often they are a response to opportunities and barriers, invitations and rejection, acceptance and marginalization.

Configuring multi-identification. In a landscape, identity is not a single process of identification, but more like a nexus of identification and dis-identification with a variety of systems, practices, and relationships. A community health worker, for example, might feel like she is a member of the practice of social care in general, but also a member of her team, an employee of her organization, a volunteer in a local voluntary nonprofit, a contributor to a blogging group about lifestyle practices. She may feel a strong connection with people she serves and their caretakers as well as some members of the mental health team, her poker group, or her family. And from some of these things, she may also feel alienated and dis-identify with them. In this nexus, she must relive and negotiate boundaries in herself. Boundaries are not just features of the landscape; they become part of people's identities.

Engaging such a health worker in an intervention must take into account her ongoing negotiation of sometimes complementary and overlapping, but often competing or conflicting loyalties. With identification comes accountability. Accountability can be formal, for example, with organizational responsibilities or legal requirements. But accountability is no less significant for being informal, for instance, loyalties to a community and its regime of competence, commitments to cultural or religious norms, as well as personal relationships to family, friends, or colleagues. Part of identity work is to manage this nexus of identification and dis-identification: find enough coherence in it over time to generate the experience of being a person.

Combining identification at multiple levels of scale. Identification often encompasses multiple levels of scale all at once. For instance, healthcare workers can identify (or dis-identify) with their patients, ward, department, hospital, region, discipline, national healthcare system. A pandemic like COVID-19 may even bring a sense of identification with all healthcare workers in the world. Resonance may be stronger at some levels than others. Some healthcare workers may identify most strongly with their hospital, some with their discipline, and some with their professional society. With some levels they may actively dis-identify, for instance, by dismissing the relevance of a national policy in practice. Many systems conveners need to do identity work across scale if they want participants to feel connected to all the dimensions of a project.

Modulating identification and dis-identification. The process of identification and dis-identification is neither determined nor fixed. For instance, people who belong to organizations, with specific missions, projects, and often-complicated politics, may identify more or less with the roles and accountability that come with their formal affiliations. Both identification and dis-identification can change with our evolving experience. Their intensity varies. New elements come in, some fade away. Identification and dis-identification strengthen or weaken over time. They become more or less salient in a given moment, depending on where we are and where we are going. Living in a landscape, we constantly modulate identification and dis-identification as we sustain and configure our identities over time.

Ideally, people participating in a systems-convening endeavor should develop an identity that matches the nature of the challenge. But systems conveners are not simply trying to create a new forms of identification shaped by their convening call. More often they are hoping for people to develop a more fluid identity, an evolving identification with multiple places in the landscape, one that is more dynamic and agile than identification with single locations or issues.[1]

---

1 From a psychological perspective, this expectation aligns with Kegan's take on the mental demands of modern life requiring people to be able to function, develop understanding and empathy, and maintain a coherent experience of self in the face of multiple competing perspectives (Kegan, 1994).

Three modes of identification

In social learning theory, the interplay between the social landscape and identity is theorized in terms of three *modes of identification:* engagement, imagination, and alignment.[1] Supporting these modes of identification can serve the practice of systems convening. We first provide brief descriptions of these three modes of identification: what they are, the tools and art of supporting them, and typical questions to drive them. Each mode has both strengths and downsides, which we mention also. The three modes work best in concert, so that they can make up for each other's shortcomings. After introducing the three modes, we explore how they can inform the various dimensions of the work of systems convening.

Engagement. By engagement we mean direct involvement in actions and interactions, either face to face or online. A central aspect of systems convening is to create occasions that promote mutual engagement, especially across boundaries.

Tools and methods. Engagement requires encounters and social spaces that invite interactions. This includes conversations, debates, and joint reflection. Engagement is also served by opportunities to do things together, engaging in practice, working on issues, and using and producing shared artifacts.

The art of engagement. We do not need to repeat the myriad of existing techniques and group activities for facilitating engagement and making creative use of physical and online spaces.[2] When facilitating boundary encounters more specifically, we follow a few heuristics. To help address issues of power, it is good to have some activities that put everyone a bit outside of their comfort zone and to set aspirations high enough that nobody has a ready-made answer to the issue at hand. In addition, we find that in boundary encounters, people need to alternate between time to engage across the boundary, and time with their home crowd to digest the implications of the boundary exploration.

Typical questions of engagement:
Q.   What are questions or issues here that we both recognize?
Q.   What does the problem look like for you?
Q.   Can you help me with this challenge?

---

1 For a more detailed description of these modes of identification, see (Wenger-Trayner, 2014).

2 See, for instance, Liberating structures, the Art of Hosting, etc.

Q.   Can we think through this question together?
Q.   How would you approach it in your practice?
Q.   What can we do together now?

Strength. Mutual engagement is a chance to partake actively in tight negotiation of meaning. The back and forth can produce mutual understanding rooted in direct experience. Engagement in joint activities can produce shared artifacts and new ideas, sometimes leading to deeper collaboration. It can give rise to deep relationships, shared memories, and even trust. Identification (or dis-identification) can be rooted in direct experience. Without moments of engagement, significant boundaries are difficult to cross or reset.

The *downside of engagement* is that it is local and limited in scope. Creating new spaces for engagement in the landscape can create new boundaries: people may build a niche of like-minded people with whom they can interact and learn, creating an insider focus and new relations of otherness beyond it. Often engagement across boundaries needs persistence and sustained interaction over time. This can be challenging to set up and maintain. In these cases, imagination and alignment can be used to open up and connect learning processes beyond a given space and to help generate commitment to a process so that participants do not to give up prematurely.

Imagination. Imagination here is not fantasy, but the ability to create images that go beyond direct experience. This includes images of the landscape through which to locate oneself; images of others, other practices, other experiences, other projects, other contexts; and new images of possible futures (and of the past beyond one's own).

Tools of imagination include stories, field trips, role plays, pictures, documentaries, maps, visuals, even games. Imagination is also triggered by building aspirational narratives, visions, and scenarios for possible futures.

The art of imagination lies in the ability to find good triggers. Central to imagination are stories and narratives. Good stories draw people in; listeners can identify with the protagonists and gain a vicarious experience of something they wouldn't know otherwise.

Typical questions of imagination:

Q.   Tell me about your context?
Q.   Am I the only one feeling this?
Q.   Where else are people doing something like this?
Q.   Have you seen what they are doing over here?
Q.   What would happen if we tried this?
Q.   What if we put ourselves in their shoes?
Q.   Where would we like to be in two years?

Strength. A social landscape is too vast and complex to gain an understanding of it through engagement alone. Many locations are relevant to what we do, but we cannot live in all of them. Imagination is therefore a necessary component of identification and dis-identification in a social landscape. Imagination can open windows that give rise to new perspectives and viewpoints. It is also a source of empathy and innovation. Without imagination, one is locked in the limitation of one's experience. It is difficult to gain a sense of the bigger picture behind what is happening or expected.

The *downside of imagination* is its very ability to detach itself from direct experience, possibly resulting in illusions, stereotypes, and assumptions. It can give rise to unrealistic aspirations, which can remain dreams and alluring narratives. By forcing a reckoning with reality, engagement and alignment can therefore act as useful checks on imagination.

Alignment. Alignment creates coordination across time and space. It is often thought of as compliance with top-down expectations, because that is often the way it is done. But we use the term more broadly. We include in the concept of alignment a two-way process between parties. Of course, when there is a significant power differential, it is easier for the powerful to demand alignment. But rebelling against a counterproductive policy is also a quest for alignment. As a mode of identification, alignment can become a deep part of a person's identity as when someone identifies with a moral code or the standards of a practice.

Tools of alignment include agreements, goals and expectation setting, division of labor, workplans, rules, codes of conduct, audits, procedures, checklists, forms, standards, legal systems, and moral frameworks.

The art of alignment. Coercion is of course a simple approach to alignment, but it is one that systems conveners tend to shy away from. They prefer convincing and forging alliances. This may require reframing purposes, negotiating expectations, and creating boundary objects that mediate alignment. Systems convening cannot ignore, but needs to work with, existing relations of accountability that participants live under: this includes offering to serve this accountability directly or indirectly, reframing it, or finding good reasons to stretch it or replace it with another.

Typical questions of alignment:

Q.   Where do our endeavors intersect?
Q.   What are you accountable to produce?
Q.   How can we coordinate what we are doing?
Q.   What's getting in the way of us doing this together?
Q.   What part of this project could you be responsible for?
Q.   How could we make this tool serve both our visions?

Strength. Alignment is necessary for combining action and achieving joint outcomes at scale. Without alignment, the lack of coordination can make local action ineffective or even counterproductive.

The *downside of alignment* is that it can easily generate or turn into compliance, where alignment replaces mutual learning and actions are performed without much understanding. Mutual engagement provides a way to negotiate and fine-tune alignment. In addition, imagination can help participants see the bigger picture and understand what alignment is meant to accomplish beyond their own contribution. Having that bigger picture allows participants to correct the course when tools of alignment fail, for instance when an instruction does not make sense.

Because these modes are complementary, they can make up for each other's downsides. Balancing their use and orchestrating their interplay for social learning can serve as a heuristic for systems convening.

Engagement, imagination and alignment in systems convening work

We have tried to summarize the implications of these modes of identification for systems convening work in the table below. For each dimension of the work, we give examples of engagement, imagination, and alignment. The first two sets of implications (convening call and legitimacy) are more for systems conveners. Implications under boundary, identity, and agency refer more to what systems conveners should be setting up and enabling for the people they are convening. The last two (power and value creation) are for both systems conveners and participants.

What it looks like in practice	Convening call	Legitimacy	Boundary
	For you, the convener.		For you to enable/
Engagement Encounters and social spaces that invite interactions, such as conversations, debates, joint reflection, doing things together, or producing shared artifacts.	Negotiate the call with people and invite them to co-develop it	Build trust through personal interaction, listening, offers of assistance, and showing understanding that reflects their perspective	Engage directly with people from other locations. Inquire into what we can do together to make a difference?
Imagination Good stories that draw people in, field trips, role plays, pictures, documentaries, maps, and visuals; building aspirational narratives, visions, and scenarios for possible futures.	Imagine what can be achieved and why other constituencies need to be included	Help people see where you are coming from and why your own journey puts you in a position to promote your vision	Imagine what others experience in their context, their aspirations, and their struggles
Alignment Agreements, setting goals and expectations, division of labor, workplans, rules, codes of conduct, audits, procedures, checklists, forms, standards, legal systems, and moral frameworks.	Have the convening call incorporate and align with demands of accountability people identify with or are subject to	Show that you understand—and can align with—what they care about or are accountable to	Take into account what others have done about the issue at hand Coordinate across boundaries to achieve common goals

Identity	Agency	Power	Value creation	
set up the conditions for participants to		For conveners and participants.		
Develop a sense of themselves and their competences in new ways by how people engage with them — or not	Be recognized as a contributor, be listened to	Have conversations with those in power to negotiate how they and you understand a situation	Have people exchange the stories of how their participation is creating value for them	**Engagement**
Understand who/ where others are in the broader landscape. Feel allegiance to communities or groups too diffuse for belonging based on interactions (e.g. lovers of a music style, citizens of a nation) Envision a new self in the future	Foresee the implications of new agency in own context	Build a picture of the power structures and politics relevant to achieving your and others' aspirations	Have people imagine how certain activities or tools might create value to make a difference that they care to make	**Imagination**
Articulate what kinds of non-negotiable aspirations, values, or principles people identify with	Seek agency within the confines of existing accountability systems. Demand that accountability systems and targets realign to include own perspective and agency.	Understand and communicate what is non-negotiable for those who have formal power and those who don't	Have people agree on aspirations for areas where creating value matters and how to monitor that	**Alignment**

A social-learning approach: cultivating social learning capability

While they may not use these words, we see systems conveners adopt a social learning approach to making a difference. Being located in a social landscape, everyone is a part of it, so no one person has a full picture of a collective endeavor. Nobody fully owns what difference to make or how to make that difference. Finding a way forward requires learning partnerships—boundary encounters, social learning spaces, communities of practice[1]—where people can learn with and from each other in pursuit of making a difference. These are participant-driven opportunities to grasp a challenge in all its authentic manifestations, negotiate what is worth striving for, and engage both their knowing and unknowing about how to get there.

Rather than managing or driving the process towards a specific change, systems conveners cultivate what we call *social learning capability* as their approach to making a difference: they work to increase the learning capability inherent in the social configuration defined by the challenge they take on. We theorize social learning capability as constituted by a dual social dynamic: the texture of entities and boundaries in the landscape and the identities that people form in relation to that texture. It is in the mutual shaping of social landscapes and identities that social learning capability exists and can be developed.[2]

To see how systems conveners cultivate social learning capability (and to clarify the concept), we can use the various dimensions of convening work we introduced earlier. Adopting a social-learning lens reveals these dimensions as attempts to enhance various aspects of social learning capability.

Convening call. Crafting, negotiating, and co-creating an aspirational narrative to inspire participation is not just a way to convey a growing understanding

---

1 For a more extensive theory of social learning spaces and their distinction from communities of practice, see (Wenger-Trayner and Wenger-Trayner, 2020)

2 The dynamics of strong ties (within entities) and weak ties (across boundaries) is well known in social network theory. For instance, adopting a social network perspective, Battilana and Casciaro distinguish between cohesive networks and bridging networks to explain the ability of organizational change agents to achieve their goal in terms of the shapes of the social networks and their positions in them (Battilana and Casciaro, 2013).

of a problem and the potential that exists in the landscape, it is also a way to develop it. Even when the convening call is adapted for different audiences, its cumulative social effect is to create a coalescing force field in the landscape. This evolving, cross-perspective view of a challenge or opportunity becomes a social container and a shared language for developing learning capability around an issue in the landscape.

Legitimacy work. The discipline of having to gain legitimacy makes for a type of leadership that is recognized as making sense to the people in its sphere. Legitimacy requires enough street creds to show a willingness to focus on authentic problems from the perspectives of people involved. It is a commitment to proceed in a way that is driven by them—not coercively manipulative or over-facilitated. But this is not enough. Legitimacy also requires a believable promise to be able to convene the right people for an actual chance at making a significant difference. The faith that participation is leading somewhere that might be better, and somewhere real, is an essential precondition for social learning capability.

Boundary work can enhance social learning capability in two ways: it can increase overall effectiveness and it can prevent groups from becoming too inward looking. On the one hand, boundary work expands learning capability from local, homogeneous locations to a broader area of the landscape by creating new learning partnerships among people who usually don't interact beyond the transactional. This expands the potential to make a difference. Working on boundaries of scale is particularly relevant to social learning capability because gaining scope by "scaling up" usually entails losing texture, and sometimes relevance. Systems, practices, and relationships often operate at different scales, with competing perspectives and priorities. Crossing boundaries of scale is a chance to inspect how actions at one level affect other levels, thereby fine-tuning the interactions between levels to be more relevant at different levels of scale.[1]

---

1 When we wrote about systems convening in 2014, we included a chapter co-authored with the leaders of the IDEA partnership, a systems-convening endeavor to help US states comply with the federal law demanding equal education for student with disabilities. One of their convening principles was to work across levels of scale: "Policymakers need to understand the effect of their policies on practice and on students. Conversely practition-ers and parents need opportunities to understand the intention behind the policies that affect them. In convening learning partnerships, we work across different levels of scale to include federal and state agencies, local districts, site leaders, practitioners, families, and youth." (Cashman et al., 2014)

On the other hand, boundary work also spurs new learning capability within the groups involved. It offers opportunities to avoid groupthink and parochialism, to rethink things, consider different perspectives, and address their implications for activities and assumptions inside groups. Whenever a challenge involves a heterogeneous set of perspectives, the ability to use boundaries as learning assets is at the core of social learning capability.

Identity work. Social learning theory is based on the assumption that learning is not only a cognitive process, but involves the whole person in a process of becoming, making meaning vis-à-vis the social landscape. Hence the emphasis on identity work. The social force of systems convening work depends on people identifying with the convening call and embracing its challenge. As it becomes part of who they are, they start developing an identity that is as "big" as the challenge. This match in size and complexity between challenge and identity is a key to social learning capability. In particular, boundaries in the landscape become reflected in people's identities. For instance, both of us (like many systems conveners we talked to) have lived large portions of our lives in different countries and cultures. The experience of these cultural boundaries has become integral part of our identities. So has the work of straddling them, including the discomfort of trying to reconcile conflicting expectations and changes in who is "other." Living a boundary in your identity makes boundary work a very personal experience. With these kinds of changes in identification, people are less likely to slip back into old behaviors; a reconfiguration of the landscape is more likely to have a lasting, transformative effect. Furthermore, people identifying with each other through convening, especially across boundaries, prepares the ground for overcoming the obstacles and differences that are bound to come up. The more people can embrace the changing landscape through a concomitant change in their identity, the more they are ready to invest themselves in the learning required. Identity work generates social and personal energy to fuel and sustain social learning capability.

Agency work can ensure a bottom-up component so that social learning capability is a combination of bottom-up and top-down forces. Creating the conditions for agency is not "anything goes" or romanticizing bottom-up processes. It is not assuming that social learning capability is only informal, organic, or emergent. But it is recognizing that there has to be a bottom-up counterpart to the top-down tendencies of most institutional systems. The interplay between the two can take many forms, ranging from full partnering to outright resistance. But without a bottom-up component in which participants experience agency, there is no social learning capability.

Power work is important because social learning capability is inevitably caught in the ongoing tension between power and learning, both at a systemic and an individual level. In social learning theory, power and learning are closely interlinked, for better and for worse. Powerfulness can move mountains, but it is often an excuse not to learn. Powerlessness forces people to adapt and find ways to survive, and therefore learn, but it also prevents this learning from making a significant or broad difference. Social learning capability has to be developed in the face of institutional systems and historical legacies that value certain voices above others and places authority and control over resources in certain hands. Changing systemic power structures is slow and difficult, but some of the problems to solve with multiple perspectives are here and now. Social learning capability lives at the cusp of this tension. Social learning capability includes a good measure of strategic shrewdness about what needs to be changed at a system level and what can be achieved within systems or at their margins. Moreover, at a practice and relationship level, the quality of the social fabric matters because social dynamics are both enablers and blockers of social learning capability. It is important to pay attention to voices, especially missing or silenced voices. Who is at the table and how they affect power dynamics make all the difference to the outcome. These dynamics can easily marginalize or even silence some voices. But what these voices have to say matters, not out of good conscience, egalitarian considerations, or good facilitation practice, but for the full learning potential of the social configuration to be achieved. Increasing social learning capability depends on an awareness and careful management of this interplay between learning and power.

Value-creation narratives. Social learning capability takes time to grow and to have a visible effect. People have to engage with each other, learn about each other, imagine their lives, discover what they mean to each other, and how they relate to the practices and systems of the landscape. It takes time to work the territory and bring everyone along. It takes time for people to develop the agency and the capacity to make a difference, both individually and collectively. Developing social learning capability is often competing with surface changes that make an impression but don't necessarily last or affect what matters. All this while there is pressure from stakeholders to show results. Playing the long game may sometimes require a certain amount of stealth. But is also requires an ability to recognize and articulate value being created at each step. At the early stages, the value may just be in the fact that people are talking to each other at all or starting to understand the situation in new ways. Some new ideas may be formed, some proposals may emerge. People may start to act differently. Until one day, a visible difference is made. Being able to articulate these different kinds of value from the start serves two purposes. It helps stakeholders and participants see the point of persevering. And it also serves learning capability by creating reflection loops: What creates value, what kind, for whom? How? What does not? Why not? What are the implications for what we are doing? Both to convey progress and to learn on the fly, the discipline of reflecting on value creation is an essential part of social learning capability.

Social learning capability is something that is anchored in people's experience as much as it is in their social context. They need to become fully engaged to bring it about. The only way to convene people authentically is to start where they are, take them as they are, and go on a joint learning journey from there. The journey has to proceed step by step, up and down, through the process of social learning, resisting the temptation to instigate or demand a quick change that assumes the social learning journey can be skipped.

Systems conveners are invested in the exploration of the difference they believe can be made; they are not consultants or facilitators brought in to take care of the process. They too have to start where they are, with their own gestating aspirations and nagging uncertainties. They learn with people, rather than make people learn. Their convening work is possible because it is a learning journey for them too. Their own experience, identity work, hopes, doubts, and learning drive are an integral part of the social learning capability they are cultivating.

5

Conclusion

We have taken a tour through the world and the work of systems conveners. We hope it has given you a sense of what they do, the challenges they face in doing it, and their own experience. And why we think it is so important.

We can see that the term could sound impressive and easily be misappropriated; we hope that we are starting to give some rigor to the claim. For us, systems conveners are an instance of what we call social learning leaders. These are people who take leadership in developing the learning capability inherent in social configurations of various sorts: communities of practice, networks, organizations, cities. In this sense, we reserve the term systems convening for the work of enhancing social learning capability in a substantial, cross-boundary area of the social landscape.

This perspective of social learning capability—and the dimensions of the work involved—is also meant to provide a framework for the discipline of systems convening. It is beginning to articulate what conveners and their sponsors need pay attention to—regarding the effectiveness and legitimacy of the convening call across constituencies, the social and personal travail of reconfiguring boundaries and identities, the attention to delicate issues of agency and power, and the process of making visible the value, sometimes obvious and often subtle, created for participants and other stakeholders. Social learning capability also depends on combining processes of engagement, imagination, and alignment and leveraging their complementarity. We hope this take on systems convening will serve the purpose of those who want to develop the practice and those who want to integrate it organizational contexts.

What we hope we have done is only a first step. It would be useful to see full case studies of systems convening, with sufficient resources to systematically monitor the short-, medium-, and long-term value that is or isn't created. Also welcomed, would be opportunities for mutual support and skill sharpening: social learning spaces, workshops, and guidebooks that provide some guidance without assuming that someone taking the approach is well versed in systems thinking, learning theory, adaptive leadership, network weaving, or any other relevant theories or adjacent practices. This would serve people embarking on making a difference guided by an intuitive sense that their endeavor involves a whole social landscape, with delicate boundaries and power dynamics; that people's identities are going to be challenged; and that much social learning will have to be enabled. It would be exciting to see these people have access to the resources they deserve.

Doing this kind of work is not going to leave you unchanged. Whether systems conveners operate alone or as a collective, their convening transforms them as well as the world. This new inquiry confirms what we observed in 2014: that systems convening is not for the faint of heart, but not for the reckless or the high-handed either; it calls for an unusual mix of boldness and humility, calculation and risk. Systems conveners are ready to take on difficult challenges, bet on people, face the resulting uncertainty, and recover from setbacks, often without much consideration for the cost to themselves. They are prepared to forge ahead, ignored, dismissed, thwarted, or even scorned by established powers. They set their sight on having their work, in the end, valued by those affected by the difference it has made. There is a kind of unspoken courage to what they do.

This brings a final observation, which seems significant, though we do not know whether it is inherent in the essence of systems convening or simply a feature of our sample so far: all the systems conveners we have encountered or worked with have had a strong moral foundation. All of them are resolute in trying to make a difference, but none of them are without scruples. This attitude may never get them to the top, perhaps, but in a time of fragmentation, their insight, initiative, and approach can achieve what may seem like small social miracles.

References

Battilana, J. and Casciaro, T. (2013) The network secrets of great change agents. *Harvard Business Review Magazine,* July-August.

Cashman, J., Linehan, P., Rosser, M., Wenger-Trayner, E., and Wenger-Trayner, B. (2014), The IDEA Partnership: convening learning partnerships in the complex landscape of special education. In Wenger-Trayner, E., Fenton-O'Creevy, M., Hutchinson, S., Kubiak, C., and Wenger-Trayner, B. (Eds.) *Learning in landscapes of practice: boundaries, identity, and knowledgeability in practice-based learning.* Routledge.

Heifetz, R., Linsky, M., and Grashow, A. (2009) *The Practice of Adaptive Leadership: Tools and Tactics for Changing Your Organization and the World.* Harvard Business Press.

Kegan, R. (1994) *In over our heads: the mental demands of modern life.* Harvard University Press.

Wenger, E. (1998) *Communities of practice: learning, meaning, and identity.* Cambridge University Press.

Wenger-Trayner, E., and Wenger-Trayner, B. (2014) Learning in landscapes of practice: a framework. In Wenger-Trayner, E., Fenton-O'Creevy, M., Hutchinson, S., Kubiak, C., and Wenger-Trayner, B. (Eds.) *Learning in landscapes of practice: boundaries, identity, and knowledgeability in practice-based learning.* Routledge.

Wenger-Trayner, E. and Wenger-Trayner, B. (2014b) Systems conveners in complex landscapes. In Wenger-Trayner, E., Fenton-O'Creevy, M., Hutchinson, S., Kubiak, C., and Wenger-Trayner, B. (Eds.) *Learning in landscapes of practice: boundaries, identity, and knowledgeability in practice-based learning.* Routledge.

Wenger-Trayner, E. and Wenger-Trayner, B. (2020) *Learning to make a difference: value creation in social learning spaces.* Cambridge University Press.

Annex

This was our invitation to interviewees

Systems convening book: interviewee profile

When we invite people for interviews, what do we mean by "systems convener" or "part of a systems convening team"? Note that systems convener is rarely the job title or even in their job description.

A systems convener or systems convening team:
- Sets up spaces for new types of conversations between people who often live on different sides of a boundary (e.g. geographic, cultural, disciplinary, political, class, social boundaries). These conveners see a social landscape with all its separate and related practices through a wide-angle lens: they spot opportunities for creating new learning spaces and partnerships that will bring different and often unlikely people together to engage in learning across boundaries.
- Takes a "landscape view" of wherever they are and what they need to do to increase the learning capability of that entire landscape—rather than simply the capability of the space they are standing in.
- Is someone who has enough legitimacy in different worlds to be able to convene people in those different worlds into a joint conversation.

Examples
- An environmental scientist brings together scientific communities, government agencies, and community organisations to learn how to translate knowledge about climate change into practice
- A Secretary of State sets up conversations between heads of states who don't normally talk to each other to solve an ongoing geopolitical problem
- A teacher sets up spaces for teachers, students and parents to see how to handle misinformation on the internet
- A social worker brings together all the different service providers (who normally don't communicate) to address a client's issues
- A hospital surgeon creates spaces for conversations and processes across different departments to develop a more rapid response to cancer diagnosis and care

By a "landscape view" we mean:

- They are knowledgeable about the various constituencies—(people in different departments, sectors, or cultures who have different identities, cultures and interests)—in the solving of a problem or in the addressing of an issue
- They are not outsiders to the issue; they have legitimacy among different constituents
- They try to change the way people on different sides of a boundary interact with each other
- A lot of their work is "identity work": getting people to identify with an issue in a new way, i.e., to identify with a larger or less homogenous group of people
- They maintain a deep awareness of their own location in the landscape and the situatedness of their work

Index

A

B

C

I

J

K

L

M

N

O

P

Q

R

S

T

U

V

W